INSIDE THE WORLD OF DIPLOMACY

INSIDE THE WORLD OF DIPLOMACY

The U.S. Foreign Service in a Changing World

Seymour M. Finger

Westport, Connecticut
London

Library of Congress Cataloging-in-Publication Data

Finger, Seymour Maxwell, 1915–
    Inside the world of diplomacy : the U.S. Foreign Service in a changing world / Seymour M. Finger.
      p. cm.
    Includes bibliographical references and index.
    ISBN 0–275–97025–6 (alk. paper)
    1. United States. Foreign Service. 2. Diplomatic and consular service, American. 3. Diplomacy. 4. United States—Foreign relations administration—History—20th century. I. Title.
    JZ1480.A4 2002
    327.73—dc21   2001034587

British Library Cataloguing in Publication Data is available.

Copyright 2002 by Seymour M. Finger

All rights reserved. No portion of this book may be reproduced, by any process or technique, without the express written consent of the publisher.

Library of Congress Catalog Card Number: 2001034587
ISBN: 0–275–97025–6

First published in 2002

Praeger Publishers, 88 Post Road West, Westport, CT 06881
An imprint of Greenwood Publishing Group, Inc.
www.praeger.com

Printed in the United States of America

The paper used in this book complies with the Permanent Paper Standard issued by the National Information Standards Organization (Z39.48–1984).

10 9 8 7 6 5 4 3 2 1

Copyright Acknowledgment

The author and publisher gratefully acknowledge permission to quote from a letter from Philip M. Klutznick to the author, December 1, 1977. With permission of James Klutznick for The Philip Klutznick estate.

This book is dedicated to my loving and deeply beloved wife, Annette. Without her gentle, persistent prodding and encouragement, it would never have been started and written. More important, she has so enriched and invigorated my life with her love, warmth, wisdom, and *joie de vivre* as to make what would have been my declining years into a time of joy, deep meaning, and fulfillment.

Contents

Preface		ix
I	A Boy Grows in Brooklyn	1
II	President Truman's Proclamation: My Entry into the Foreign Service	5
III	Embassy Paris	9
IV	Behind the Iron Curtain—Budapest	13
V	The Harvard Interlude and Rome	17
VI	Life in Laos	21
VII	Life in the Big Time: Henry Cabot Lodge and the United Nations	27
VIII	Adlai Stevenson	47
IX	Arthur J. Goldberg: A Justice Comes to the UN	91
X	Charles Yost and the Nixon-Kissinger Years	127
XI	George Bush—A Future President at the UN	141

XII	Life after the Foreign Service	149
XIII	A Foreign Service for the 21st Century	155
Bibliography		159
Index		163

Preface

A satirical definition holds: "A diplomat is someone sent abroad to lie for his country." It reflects a popular misconception. In my 26 years as an American diplomat I found that lying is the worst way to carry out effective diplomacy. Once duplicity is revealed and a reputation for integrity is lost, a diplomat becomes useless or worse.

Another misperception is that the U.S. Foreign Service is made up of rich young men from Ivy League colleges who spend most of their time on high living abroad. There may have been some basis for that perception before World War II, but certainly not since then. Entry into the Foreign Service is based on extremely difficult written and oral examinations. When I took the exams in 1946, only about 7 percent passed. Now I believe the figure is closer to 2 percent. Of course, no test can guarantee performance, but I found my Foreign Service colleagues to have exceptional ability and integrity.

Also, they represented a cross-section of America—different religions and races, varied financial circumstances, graduates of universities across the country, some from law schools—but alike in ability and dedication. My own background was that of a Jewish boy who grew up in Brooklyn. My father died when I was three, and I did all the "Horatio Alger" jobs from the age of eight—selling and delivering newspapers, peddling bananas, selling magazine subscriptions door-to-door—certainly not the popular image of an American diplomat.

Graduating from Ohio University during the Great Depression at age nineteen with the ambition of becoming a professor of American history,

I was unable to get a teaching job. In need of money for myself, a widowed mother, and a sister, I took a job as branch manager for a major chain of photograph studios. From there I went into the Army in February 1943 as a Volunteer Officer Candidate and served in the battles of Normandy, Northern France, the Ardennes, and the Rhine. I then passed the exam for the Foreign Service and was appointed Vice Counsel at Stuttgart in February 1946. I rose through the various ranks until my appointment as Ambassador at the U.S. Mission to the United Nations (UN) in 1967.

In my boyhood days, I never dreamed that one day I would be involved in developing American programs and policies that would have a significant impact on the United States and the world. Nor did I imagine that I would be working closely with prominent figures like Henry Cabot Lodge, Adlai Stevenson, Arthur Goldberg, Paul Hoffman, Eleanor Roosevelt, and George Bush in the conception, development, and implementation of these policies. Now, in my "senior years," I have decided to record the inside story of those exciting years in a memoir.

Most of these high-level contacts concerned with policy making occurred during fifteen years with the U.S. Mission to the United Nations. I was, successively, Senior Economic Advisor, Minister-Counselor, and Ambassador. I was involved in initiating the Special Fund, which became the UN Development Program and is now the world's largest program of technical assistance ($2 billion per year). At Lodge's request, I drafted an outline for the World Food Program, which he passed directly to President Eisenhower. It became the basis of a U.S. initiative at the UN, where I helped to present it and gain the approval of the General Assembly. The World Food Program now helps millions of people around the world.

My story will also deal with the give-and-take between the U.S. Mission and Washington in the formulation of policies as well as the role of the Mission in carrying those policies forward at the UN. Contrary to the popular perception that oratory wins votes, it is one-on-one contacts that are most important. Maintaining good relations with over a hundred delegations is time-consuming and makes for a long working day, normally twelve hours. In the crisis leading up to the Six-Day War, the war itself, and its aftermath, we worked a fourteen-hour day, seven-day week for three months.

Our brilliant chief, Arthur Goldberg, led our team in an effort that turned around a majority of the membership from an anti-Israel stance to one that was fair to both the Arabs and the Jews. It was embodied in Resolution 242 of the Security Council, the only basis on which Israel and its Arab neighbors have agreed to negotiate peace. An insider's account of that struggle will, I am sure, be of interest.

Goldberg's role illustrates another important point that my story will develop, i.e., that dedicated, forceful individuals have a major impact in making American policy. They lead and move a massive bureaucracy that might otherwise remain inert. Also, being involved with such a leader who is close to the President gives one an opportunity to promote significant ideas.

My book will also deal with my five assignments abroad, in Stuttgart, Paris, Budapest, Rome, and Vientiane, Laos. These afforded fascinating experiences, learning new languages, cultures, and systems. I take particular pride in a report I wrote in Budapest, analyzing the Hungarian Five-Year Plan of that period. It showed clearly how far below the published figures was the actual production of key items, such as steel and food. It was the first analysis of its kind that the State Department had ever received. In a way it foreshadowed the collapse of the Soviet system three decades later. I plan to tell how the report was put together, using the published sources and interviews, without resorting to espionage or agents. This function of observation, analysis, and reporting can be highly important in shaping foreign policy.

In addition to dealing with these successful efforts, I shall also describe my failures and shortcomings as a diplomat, and provide an insider's evaluation of the various diplomats with whom I worked.

I hope my story will encourage other young men and women, including those of modest circumstances, to try for the Foreign Service. We need the best, and competition will help keep standards high. Secretary of State Madeline Albright expressed it well: "Just as we have a world-class military, we must have world-class diplomacy." It is perhaps not sufficiently appreciated that many world conflicts have been successfully averted by intelligent, sensitive diplomacy. Our fervent hopes for world peace may find one important source in principled and enlightened diplomacy.

I hope my book will reveal to the general reader some instances of the above, under the leadership of diplomats whom I had the privilege to observe firsthand. At the same time I hope the reader will find this inside story of American diplomacy a good and interesting read.

Seymour M. Finger

CHAPTER I

A Boy Grows in Brooklyn

My father died when I was three. A young man of 32, he was carried off in the flu epidemic of 1918.

I have few personal memories of my father, just a vague recollection of having gone with him to the barbershop. From what others have said, he must have been a man of unusual intelligence, ambition, and energy. Arriving in the United States alone at age nineteen from what was then Austria, he managed in thirteen years to build a highly successful business for the wholesale distribution of fruits and vegetables. He was greatly respected in the family; I am proud to bear his genes. My mother and relatives say I look like him, and pictures seem to bear that out.

Like many successful immigrants, my father became an avid American patriot. My mother told me that it was his dream for my brother, three years older, to go to West Point and for me to attend Annapolis. Neither one of us went in that direction, but I like to think he would have been proud of our service in the U.S. Army in World War II and my subsequent career in the U.S. Foreign Service.

Though deprived of my father, I was fortunate in having my mother's complete, unconditional love. This she gave me until the end of her life at age 80. She had been born and brought up on New York's Lower East Side, then a haven for Jewish immigrants. Her parents had come from Hungary, where her two older brothers were born. Her mother had insisted on leaving Hungary out of fear that her boys would be drafted into the Austro-Hungarian army. Apparently I did inherit my father's drive and mind. In spite of certain discipline problems in elementary school, I advanced rapidly, finishing the normal eight-year program in six years. In those days bright children in the New York City schools could skip grades, and I scored in the 150s on the IQ test. It was only later that the concept of enrichment programs without skipping took hold.

Upon graduation from Boys High School in Brooklyn, I decided to go to college out of town rather than to a city college. I loved Ohio University, then a small institution with 2,500 students in Athens, a little town of 5,000 in the rural southeast of Ohio. There was no pressure to perform, but a fine faculty and a wonderful library where I did virtually all of my studying. It came almost as a surprise when I was eligible for Phi Beta Kappa in my junior year and made it. I was also on the debating team, which offered dual rewards: the stimulus of debate and the opportunity to travel to other colleges around the state. I could not afford much for food and loved the steak dinners when we traveled, with the University picking up the tab.

When I graduated in January 1935, my prospects were dim. The economy was still depressed. I wanted to teach American history or mathematics, my two college majors, but midyear was not a good time to get a teaching job. Also, I was nineteen and looked it, and that apparently did not go well with prospective employers. I applied for a job cleaning up a bakery, but was turned down as being "overqualified." I went back to selling magazine subscriptions door-to-door but that was no fun in the February cold of New York. My goal became getting a job where I could earn a living indoors.

Fortunately I soon landed a job with the American Photograph Corporation which had chains of over 200 photograph studios operating in leading department stores all over the country. After training, I successively became the manager of studios in Fort Wayne, Miami, Atlanta, St. Louis, and Cincinnati, each one somewhat larger than its predecessor. Cincinnati was the second largest branch in the chain, and there I was given the job of training prospective managers.

I took one of them to lunch to discuss problems he was having with the job. Halfway through lunch he said: "You know, you ought to be in the diplomatic service." That started me thinking. My first thought was that the diplomatic service would be too "highfalutin" for someone of my background, but perhaps I could fit in the consular service. When I wrote to Washington I learned that both were part of the U.S. Foreign Service. This chance remark was a decisive factor in my choice of a lifetime career.

In the meantime the United States, after the Japanese bombed Pearl Harbor, entered World War II. I joined the Army as a Volunteer Officer Candidate and was assigned to the Signal Corps. When I finished basic training I was told that the Signal Corps had all the officers it needed and I had the option of returning to civilian life. I learned, however, that the Army was training French liaison teams, and, on the basis of three years of high school French and a lot of nerve, I was accepted for that program

A Boy Grows in Brooklyn

where I really learned the language. Additionally, later while serving in the Army in Germany in the last months of the war I brought my high school German up to fluency.

I also had an opportunity to study history and international law as preparation for the Foreign Service. My Army unit was in the battles of Normandy and northern France. Then four of us were despatched to Luxembourg during the Battle of the Bulge to run the Luxembourg communications network (which had become the Third Army Network) supervising local technicians. We had fluent French and some knowledge of telecommunications. At first we would be on duty for 24 hours, sleep for six hours, and go back on duty. Lines were constantly being shot out or bombed out and we had to find alternate routing. But in time the Germans retreated, the front moved away, and we could be on duty for twelve hours and off for 24. This gave me the opportunity to study for long hours at the library in preparation for the Foreign Services exam.

From there we moved to Germany and I wound up the war in Berlin, going home for discharge in November 1945.

CHAPTER II

President Truman's Proclamation: My Entry into the Foreign Service

I was feeling frustrated about the Foreign Service. I now had fluent French and German and had done a lot to prepare myself. But I learned that the age limit for the examination was 30, and I would be two months over age for the next one. I had also been jolted by an interview with the American Consul in Frankfurt. I was wearing my sergeant's uniform. He was of the old school, the Foreign Service that had recruited rich young men from "good families." He asked critically, "What makes you think you're fit for the Foreign Service? Have you got any money?"

I was rescued by an act of President Truman. On December 22, 1945, he issued a directive to facilitate immigration into the United States for Holocaust survivors. It was an act of great compassion and courage. There was much opposition to immigration in the United States. Consuls were authorized to accept a corporate affidavit guaranteeing that the immigrant would not become a public charge. Previously the affidavit had to be made by an individual. It was very difficult and time-consuming to find an individual sponsor for each immigrant. Under Truman's proclamation an organization like the American Joint Distribution Committee or the Hebrew Immigrant Aid Society (HIAS) could provide thousands of corporate affidavits and subsequently transfer the responsibility to a willing individual sponsor.

Truman emphasized the need to act expeditiously to set up consular offices near the survivors to relieve their suffering. As a result there was a need for many more consular officers than the Foreign Service could provide, and a group of us were appointed as noncareer vice-consuls, with no assurance of permanent appointment. But we were permitted to take the career Foreign Service examination, waiving the 30-year age limit.

My appointment came in an amusing way. I was working in New York when a call came to the candy store beneath my mother's Brooklyn apartment that Mr. Burns of the State Department wanted to speak to Mr. Finger. At that time James Byrnes was Secretary of State. My mother, who was never modest about my talents, assumed that the Secretary of State had made the wise decision to hire her Seymour to rescue the country. When I called back to the number indicated, Mr. Burns turned out to be Findley Burns, a personnel officer in the State Department. He offered me a job as a noncareer vice-consul, and I happily accepted. So on January 31, 1946, I was back in Germany!

My flight to Germany was on an American Airlines propeller plane. We had to stop in Gander, Newfoundland, to refuel and again in Shannon, Ireland, en route to Frankfurt. We took the train from Frankfurt to Stuttgart, passing through a heavily bombed, thoroughly devastated Mannheim. Stuttgart, whose main industry was machine tools rather than heavy industry, had suffered much less.

My job in Stuttgart was challenging. In my first year I interviewed Holocaust survivors who wanted visas for the United States. It was not easy. Ordinarily an applicant would present a birth certificate, as proof of his identity and place of birth, as well as a police record. These survivors had no documents; all had been destroyed. We had to decide on the basis of an application form and an interview whether the applicant was qualified to enter the United States.

To be truthful, the attitude of vice-consuls varied. Some had been immigration officers on the Mexican border, and they generally had a negative attitude toward all immigrants. Nevertheless, they did their job faithfully and issued hundreds of visas. As the son of an immigrant, I naturally had a more sympathetic attitude, but not an uncritical one. I must have issued over two thousand visas that year and, to the best of my knowledge, none of the recipients wound up in prison. Subsequently, I saw many of them in the United States, holding responsible jobs and raising families.

The decision on entry to the United States placed a heavy responsibility on us. Many Nazi collaborators, especially those from the Baltic states, tried to pose as survivors of Nazi persecution, and we had to weed them out. On the other hand, denying a visa to a true victim of Nazi persecution could have a devastating effect on a life. Consequently, I weighed every decision with the greatest of care.

As part of the process, the applicant had to answer about 30 questions orally, under oath. Lying on these questions can be the basis for deportation. Most of the applicants were Jewish and spoke Yiddish. I did not know Yiddish but asked the questions in German, which was close enough to

Yiddish for them to understand. Occasionally, I would throw in a few Yiddish words I knew, and they loved it.

I got to know a lot about them by frequent visits to the Displaced Persons (DP) camp, which was run by a friend, Lou Levitan. Thus, I could tell who was on the level.

Our closest friends in the consulate were Roy and Betty Atherton. Roy was a particularly admirable person and had a distinguished career in the Foreign Service, winding up as Ambassador to Egypt. (He was on the reviewing stand, a few feet away, when Anwar Sadat was assassinated.) A Harvard graduate, he has a superb mind, complete integrity, a total absence of self-importance, and a delightful sense of humor.

In the fall of 1946 I took the exam for the career Foreign Service and passed it. It is a very difficult, competitive exam, consisting of a written and an oral part. That year 20 percent passed the written exam. In the orals, two-thirds of those were eliminated, so that only 7 percent of the applicants were appointed. I understand that the percentage passing in recent years has been even lower. A shortage of funds has limited the number of new appointments.

The written exam tests the breadth and understanding of your reading, your ability to analyze complex material, and your skill in writing clearly under time pressure. These are all skills important to the job itself.

The orals are geared to test your ability to express yourself orally and to see how you react under pressure. Since I had majored in American history, one examiner (there are five) proceeded to ask very detailed questions until he came to one I could not answer. The purpose here was not to test my knowledge but rather to see how I could handle the embarrassment of not knowing the answer in my special field. Another examiner asked my views on the question of Palestine, then a British mandate. I am sure that was because he knew I was Jewish and wanted to see whether I was emotionally biased on the issue. I must have done all right, as I got appointed.

Following my year of visa work in Stuttgart, I was given the job of political reporting on southwest Germany (Württemberg-Baden). There was still no federal republic of Germany, so the various consulates were given a function in their area that is normally carried out by an embassy.

I enjoyed the job enormously. I could read and speak German, had many sources of information, and came to know the influential politicians in the area. Also, I wrote short biographies of some of the leading personalities who later became important in the Federal Republic: e.g., President Theodor Heuss and Reinhold Meier. The task was greatly facilitated by the availability of *fragebogen*, the detailed questionnaires that all Germans had to fill out as part of the denazification process. Starting with that information, it was relatively easy to build a good biography by using other documentary information, newspaper clippings, and personal interviews.

With the establishment of the German Federal Republic in 1948 and the setting up of a U.S. Embassy in Bonn, the job of political and economic reporting went to the Embassy. But the groundwork laid by the consulates before that time provided a very useful base for continued analysis.

We had home leave in the summer of 1948, during the crisis over the Soviet blockade of Berlin. As is frequently the case, we found people in the United States much more concerned and excited by that crisis than we were.

CHAPTER III
Embassy Paris

In May 1949 came a transfer to the American Embassy in Paris, a city I had loved since my first contact in 1944. I was also promoted from Third Secretary to Second Secretary. I was assigned to the Economic Section, with responsibility for the monthly economic review and the textile, leather, and hides and skins industries. These industries were of special concern to the United States, which supplied raw cotton to French textile manufacturers and bought French calfskins for shoe uppers and horse butts for baseballs. The French leather manufacturers wanted to minimize exports so that an abundant supply in France would tend to depress prices. The dealers in hides and skins, on the other hand, wanted exports as a way of earning dollars abroad and improving their bargaining position in France. Of course I was their ally, on behalf of the American leather industry. On returning to the United States I was given a token award by the Tanners Council of America (a leather wallet).

In Paris I shared an office and a secretary with Rupert Lloyd, an African-American Foreign Service Officer (FSO) who had just spent eight years at the American Embassy in Liberia. This was at a time when black FSOs were routinely assigned to either Liberia or Haiti, before the explosion of independence in Africa.

Rupert's assignment to Paris was a sign that this unfortunate policy was finally being terminated. He was a superb choice. He was completely fluent in French, well steeped in French culture, and had done his Ph.D. dissertation on Anatole France. Understandably, he was very popular with the

French. He also had a delicious sense of humor and a marvelous belly laugh.

But there was a somber side to Rupert. He had felt many lashes of race prejudice in his native Virginia. When his father, a physician, developed an illness that proved to be terminal, the local hospital would not admit him because of his color. Rupert also told of a little neighbor girl, white, who visited their home. There were pictures of Rupert and his brother, who was blond and blue-eyed, on the piano. Pointing to his brother, she said, "He's beautiful." She then pointed to Rupert's picture and said, "But I don't like that one. He looks like a nigger." Such incidents had made Rupert bitter. At one point Rupert asked me, "Max, do you think it's an accident that they put the nigger and the Jewboy together?" In any case we became friends and often made up a foursome.

As a junior officer in Paris I had few entertainment obligations. About once every two months I had to show up for the Ambassador's reception. He had to hold many, to show courtesy to the hordes of visitors who came to Paris. However, the entertainment allowance would come close to being exhausted shortly after the mammoth 4th of July party, attended by virtually all Americans who lived in Paris and many, many visitors. This left only limited funds for receptions until the end of the year. Fortunately, our Ambassador at the time was David Bruce, a man who was independently wealthy and superbly qualified to be Ambassador to Paris. He spoke excellent French, knew the country very well, and was highly intelligent, well-informed, and a superb diplomat. As an added bonus he had an excellent cellar of marvelous French wines. His wife, Evangeline, herself the daughter of an Ambassador, was beautiful, gracious, elegant, and highly cultured. Would that all our noncareer Ambassadors were so highly qualified!

We junior officers had three main functions in a well-orchestrated reception that ran from 6 P.M. to 8 P.M. Some of us would greet the guests at the door, then introduce them to the Bruces in a loud, clear voice, before going back to the door to pick up new guests. Others would steer guests away from the receiving line toward the beverages and hors d'oeuvres, to make sure the line kept moving. Others would socialize with the people who already had their drinks. At ten minutes to eight we would begin shaking hands ostentatiously and saying goodnight to the Ambassador and Mrs. Bruce as a signal that it was time to go. By 8 P.M. the party was over.

My social life was not limited to these evening functions, as I was frequently entertained at lunch by French businessmen or officials, though always at a restaurant. The French appeared to make it a point to separate their private lives from their business.

Good wine and good food seemed to be therapeutic for the French. I recall one day when the United States announced a substantial cut in the allocation of raw cotton for the French. One of my textile industry contacts called up and asked whether I was free for dinner, and I was. I met him and ten or eleven others at Maxim's. They were a sad bunch. But as the meal progressed and we drank good wine, I could see their spirits rising. By the end of the meal they were recalling other crises they had surmounted and vowing to surmount this one. And they did! It was also clear that I liked them and they liked me and we would work together for the best possible outcome.

Another job I had, in addition to my assigned functions as an economic officer, was that of Weekend Duty Officer. This meant representing the U.S. government to Americans in Paris and to French officials, and my weekend involved some very interesting cases.

First, I had a phone call from a distraught American mother whose son had moved in with a French woman whom she considered immoral and very bad for her son. Could the Embassy break up the affair and force him to move out? Regretfully, I had to inform her that our authority did not extend to that sort of situation.

The next phone call was from the French police. It concerned a black American prize fighter named "Dynamite" Jefferson who had gotten drunk in a Paris cafe and proceeded to punch other patrons and smash furniture. Understandably, the French had decided to deport him. They were afraid that he might act up en route to Le Havre and that he might be hurt in the process of subduing him. I told the police we could not take custody on French soil; consequently, they would have to deal with the problem of escorting him outside the country. The police officer thanked me politely, and sighed.

On the next situation I was able to be more helpful. An American diplomat in Yugoslavia had come down with a serious illness for which the indicated medicines were not available in that country. I was able to procure the medicines at a Paris pharmacy and deliver them to the conductor of the Orient Express for delivery to Belgrade, where an Embassy officer picked them up.

There were a few other incidents that weekend, including a phone call about an American girl who had played strip poker and lost everything. Fortunately, she was covered and escorted home by friends.

CHAPTER IV

Behind the Iron Curtain—Budapest

When I learned that I was assigned to Budapest, I wondered how to break the news to my mother. She asked where I would like to go for my next post and I told her I thought I'd like Moscow. I thought I could then gradually edge toward Budapest. But she said: "Moscow! Look what happened to Vogeler." As it happened, Vogeler, an AT&T (American Telephone & Telegraph) official, was imprisoned in Budapest! In any case, she gradually got used to the idea and brought up the subject of her parents, who had immigrated from Hungary. She taught me a few words of Hungarian, none of which could be used in polite company.

Budapest proved to be a most challenging assignment. When I arrived in 1951, Stalin was still in power and Hungary was being run in the Soviet image. Living conditions were awful, and the bulk of the people hated the regime. It was not only repressive, but its leaders had spent the war in Moscow and returned in the wake of Soviet tanks. They were considered mere puppets of Moscow, which indeed they were. There was also an ethnic factor. Seven of the ten top Communists were Jewish, including the leader, Matyas Rakosi, and deputy, Erno Gero. They were not considered true Magyars.

The presence of Jews among the leaders in the East European Communist countries was widespread, e.g., Jakob Berman in Poland, Ana Pauker in Rumania, Rudolph Slansky in Czechoslovakia. This may be explained by the situation of Eastern Europe in the 1930s when, outside of Czechoslovakia, repressive right-wing dictatorships prevailed. The main organized opposition groups were the Communists. Many idealistic young Jews, opposed to the right-wing oppression, gravitated toward them.

The situation in Stalinist Hungary was particularly hard for the small Jewish merchants. As merchants, they were despised by the Communist authorities. As Jews, they were hated by the majority, which felt oppressed by the Jewish Communist leadership.

My own identity with the Hungarian authorities was that of an American diplomat, hated and distrusted as an instrument of the world's most powerful capitalist nation. For two years they recorded every phone call I made and followed my car wherever I went. On the other hand, the ordinary Hungarians were eager to be friendly. They still had a hope that American tanks would roll into Hungary and set them free—a vain hope, as the 1956 Revolution demonstrated.

My job as economic officer was unusually challenging and rewarding. Besides the normal periodic reporting, I embarked on a comprehensive analysis of the Hungarian economy, to determine how their economy was really doing, in contrast to the official reports that appeared in the press. I had a great stroke of luck in finding that a Hungarian employed as translator by the military attaché had a long career as a mining engineer. He knew every coal mine in Hungary and was able to make a reliable estimate of coal production. No coal was being imported. Since he knew exactly how much coal was required to make a ton of steel, we were able to make a reliable estimate of steel production. It proved to be about two-thirds of the official figure put out by the government. By careful reading of the technical journals and conversations with the engineer, Herczeg, I was able to make reliable estimates in many other areas. It soon became clear that the official figures put out by the government were essentially for propaganda purposes and had no reliable relationship to reality. My conclusions also demonstrated the inefficiency of the communist economy, predating by several decades Gorbachev's revelations about Soviet inefficiency.

I had started my analysis in February, estimating that it would take two or three months. I wound up finishing it in August, just before the end of my assignment. Washington had not requested such a comprehensive analysis, but I thought it was important to do it on the basis of my experience and the contacts I had, along with my ability to read some Magyar. (I took lessons while I was there.) A new man coming in would require many months to familiarize himself with the situation. Meanwhile, good sources might dry up. So I wound up in the office frequently on Saturday and Sunday, often working in my underwear shorts in the hot August weather.

During the spring, I had checked up on the crops by forays in the countryside. I also walked through the food markets and was able to predict a serious food shortage.

It was worth all the effort. My report was the first comprehensive analysis of an Eastern European Communist Five-Year Plan that the State Department had received. As I found out on home leave, when it was suggested that I see "the boys across the street" it was made available to the Central Intelligence Agency (CIA). Subsequent announcements by a post-Rakosi government criticized him for producing inaccurate reports of production and tended to come out with figures much like those I had arrived at. I was so excited by the results that I wanted to become a specialist on the Soviet bloc; however, State Department and family considerations turned me in other directions.

Living conditions in Budapest were very good for diplomats, in contrast with the miserable lot of most Hungarians. We were well housed, the climate was good, and the Hungarian servants were superb. At the French Minister's home, you were served delicious French food, at the Italian's wonderful Italian food, etc., all prepared by talented Hungarian cooks.

The social life was frantic. The wives, who generally did not work, were panicked by the fact that you could not have meaningful relations with Hungarians. If you saw a Hungarian who was not your employee several times, the likelihood was that he would either be put in prison or made to work for the Secret Police. In good conscience you did not want to expose them to these dangers. The result was a great deal of social inbreeding, i.e., diplomats seeing other diplomats at dinners most evenings. When it became difficult to make interesting conversation with the same people, a custom developed to play bridge or show a movie borrowed from the U.S. army in Vienna. Of course, the diplomats exchanged information and thoughts during the day and with cigars after dinner.

Early in my stay in Hungary I was asked to occupy the residence of the Minister, pending his arrival. I remember driving my little Hillman Minx up the driveway, to be met by a staff of six servants standing at attention. As I approached them the lights went on. It reminded me of a scene from *Sunset Boulevard* when the young man arrives at the mansion of the former movie queen.

After the Minister arrived I moved to an apartment on the Danube, at Szechenyi Rakpart. It was quite comfortable, with a balcony overlooking the river. I shared a cook with Bill Balazs, our Political Officer. Bill came from a Hungarian family in Cleveland and spoke Magyar fluently. He was modest, witty, and bright and did a great job of political reporting. It was only many years later, after we had both retired, that I learned he worked for the CIA. Usually I could spot the CIA types, and most were not nearly as bright and effective as Bill.

My closest buddy, however, was Pat O'Sheel, the representative of the U.S. Information Agency. Pat was brilliant, sardonic, and sometimes too outspoken. He was a shrewd judge of people and could penetrate phoniness quickly and surely. We spent many a Saturday afternoon wandering around the art shops of Budapest.

Another man I felt close to was our new Minister, Christian Ravndal.

Chris was a man of insight, charm, and boldness, a great boss. He and I hit it off very well; subsequently, when he was Ambassador to Ecuador, he asked for me to be assigned there, but my then boss, Henry Cabot Lodge, wanted to retain me. Since he was close to President Eisenhower, he was able to veto any transfer. An active man by nature, he was frustrated by how little real negotiation or business could be done with the Hungarian government at that time. His frustration was further intensified when the authorities closed down the only golf course in the country.

Perhaps the most exciting single incident during my two years in Budapest was the forcing down of a U.S. Army supply plane that had blundered over Hungarian airspace en route from Frankfurt to Belgrade. The Hungarian government called it a spy plane and imprisoned the crew of four. After many months of negotiation we got them out by paying a fine of $120,000.

Another major event was the death of Joseph Stalin early in 1953. There was then some improvement in our relations with the Hungarian officials. At receptions the Soviet bloc diplomats, who had always formed a solid phalanx around the food, began to circulate and talk to Western diplomats. Usually the subjects were innocuous, like the weather, but at least there was human contact.

There was also some loosening up of travel restrictions. Except for the road to Vienna, we were not allowed to travel more than 25 kilometers from the center of Budapest without a special permit, which was not usually forthcoming. There would not be an outright denial, but if the permit did not come by Friday evening you knew you were not going. Still, we tested every week by filing applications. Finally, in April 1953, a group of us got permission to visit Lake Balaton, Hungary's largest. After so much anticipation, the lake was a disappointment. It is surrounded by flat land and most of it is shallow. You can walk in about 75 yards, and the water would still be only up to your waist.

In one situation I decided to deal with the problem by use of the Hungarian Communist technique of not responding. My Hungarian assistant, Dr. Gal, was picked up by the police and imprisoned. When Hungarian exporters came with documents to be authenticated, I told them we could not do it because we were short of staff. This meant that they could not export to the United States. After a few days they apparently got the message. Gal was released, came back to work, and we resumed authenticating documents. He was not bothered after that, as least during my stay in Hungary.

CHAPTER V

The Harvard Interlude and Rome

After almost eight years in service abroad, I was eligible for midcareer training either at the Foreign Service Institute in Washington or at a university. I chose to do graduate work in economics at Harvard and was accepted. I felt strongly then, and still do, that anyone engaged in international politics should at least be literate in economics. In my undergraduate days in the early 1930s I had taken only one semester of economics and decided that the course, as taught, was worthless. We were being taught that equilibrium would come about automatically during any recession or depression. All around us was evidence of a deep, four-year-old depression, with no sign of recovery or "equilibrium."

Fortunately, economics as taught at Harvard in 1953–1954 was completely different. There was a brilliant faculty, including people like John Kenneth Galbraith, Gotfried Haberler, Alvin Hansen, and John Williams. I took a course in money and banking, taught jointly by Hansen and Williams, and I learned a great deal about how an economy functions. Hansen was a leading Keynesian, Williams a pragmatist who served on the board of the Federal Reserve Bank of New York; they were good foils for each other.

Under the terms of my assignment, which paid not only my tuition but also my salary for the nine months at Harvard, I was allowed to take only two courses per semester for credit, but there was no limit on the number of courses I could audit. In fact, I audited six courses each semester, in addition to the two I took for credit. It meant being involved night and day, with only Saturday night reserved for fun, but I was determined to get the most out of my time there.

In the second semester I wanted to audit a course on "The Legal Aspects of International Organization." When I saw Richard Gardner, one of the two law professors running the course, he told me it was a small seminar that I could attend only if I took it for credit. I did, and had no regrets. The seminar, taught jointly by Gardner and Harold Berman, another law school professor, was intriguing at every session. Also, I was required to do a paper, which became my first publication. I did a study of the Escape Clause in U.S. commercial policy, delving into each case that was brought up in an attempt to restrict foreign competition. I learned about garlic, spring clothespins, and pregnant mares' urine (used to produce estrogen). My conclusion was that the Escape Clause was unnecessary and obstructive. Gardner showed the paper to Haberler and Galbraith, editors of *Public Policy*, and they agreed to publish it in that journal.

Gardner and I were to be involved again with each other years later. In 1961, in the Kennedy Administration he became Deputy Assistant Secretary of State for International Organization (I.O.). I was then Senior Economic Adviser at the U.S. Mission to the UN which came under the jurisdiction of I.O., as we called it. Dick and I worked closely together on the UN Development Decade, the World Food Program, and the UN Conference on Trade and Development. He was a brilliant young man whose education included Harvard, Oxford (Rhodes Scholar), and Yale Law School. When still in his twenties he wrote a classic book, *Sterling-Dollar Diplomacy*.

I rented a room in a house near the Harvard campus and had good neighbors, all academics. They were shocked when State Department investigators asked them questions about my lifestyle and habits. Did I bring home guests? Did any stay the night? Were they male or female? I think the only damaging testimony at that time would have been if I had male guests spending the night. Homosexuals were then being hounded out of the Foreign Service, as part of the McCarthy era. In any case, I got my promotion, which was the reason for the investigations. Unaware of its purpose, my academic neighbors had been far more shocked by it than I was. As my stay at Harvard came to a close, I started thinking about my next assignment. I hoped that it would be somewhere in the Soviet bloc or Berlin, as I had become fascinated with that area during my time in Hungary. Instead, I was assigned to the Embassy in London. I thought, "Not bad. I can renew acquaintances with some of the British friends I made in Budapest." (Our two legations worked very closely together.) I ordered a right-hand drive Chevrolet to be delivered in London. Then, a week before I had to leave, a personnel officer called me up and asked whether I would like to go to Rome. At that time I preferred London, but how could I reject a place like Rome? My order for a Chevrolet was changed to a left-hand drive to be delivered to Rome.

Immediately on arriving I had started studying Italian. It has always seemed to me that you lose at least half the flavor of a country if you don't speak the language. I found it easier to think in French and then translate into Italian because the structure of the two languages was very similar. English, on the other hand, has a very different structure. By the end of three months I was speaking a serviceable Italian and reading it without difficulty.

My job title was Economic Defense Officer. This meant keeping track of Italian trade with the Soviet bloc to find evidence that the allied list of forbidden items was being violated. The list had been agreed to in NATO and was under the general authority of its coordinating committee (CO-COM). We kept in close touch with Italian officials who were responsible for monitoring the trade and they were very cooperative. We never succeeded in eliminating all such trade, but our joint efforts helped to reduce it.

CHAPTER VI

Life in Laos

After only nine months, my Roman idyll ended. I was transferred to the American Embassy in Vientiane, Laos, a victim of Secretary Dulles's traveling habits. After the French agreed in Geneva in 1954 to leave all of Indochina, Dulles surveyed Vietnam, Cambodia, and Laos to see what the United States could do in the situation. He was determined to stop the Communist advance but not sure how.

When Dulles's plane arrived over Laos it had to circle for 20 minutes so that the water buffalo could be cleared off the runway. At the Embassy he found that the only person who could speak French was Ambassador Yost, who was down with amebic dysentery. He sent a cable to Washington stating that he wanted a middle-level officer fluent in French for Laos at once and it would not matter where he was or what he was doing. Apparently three cards dropped out of the sorting machine. The other two officers were in Washington and had chiefs who successfully argued that they were indispensable; I had no such support, and went to Laos, not very happily.

Vientiane was really an overgrown village, suddenly become the capital of a new country. Buffalo were often seen on the main street and the paved road ended about two miles from the center of town. In the rainy season when the rivers were at their crest, you could not go by land from Vientiane to any of the other provinces.

The French had not built much in the way of amenities. There was not a single swimming pool in the whole country and certainly not a golf course. Vietnam and Cambodia, with access to the sea, were far more interesting commercially. Consequently, the French presence in Laos was very limited. Laos had no significant exports and its buying power was minimal. Evidently the French left Laos much as they had found it a century earlier. They had a second layer of officials who were Vietnamese. These were the people Lao hated and feared, not the French, with whom the Lao had little direct contact. Their main impact was that the educated class of Lao, who ran the country, spoke French. That was why I was there.

Living accommodations were also limited. I lived in a bedroom in a house with Wendell Blancke, the Deputy Chief of Mission, and his wife, Frances. Wendell had also arrived as a reinforcement after the Dulles visit. I had known and liked him immensely when we were both serving in Germany. He was an extraordinary man in many ways—full of wit, intelligence, and humor. He had been working as Art Director for the J. Walter Thompson Agency in Argentina when World War II broke out. Since he knew the country and the language so well, the Embassy coopted him for the duration of the war. When the war ended, he was assigned to Berlin and I got to know him during his visits to Stuttgart.

Completely fluent in Spanish, German, and French, Wendell was a marvelous raconteur. He also composed verses and music with great talent. He knew serious music well enough so that he could play around with it. Wendell also ran our household very well, with the help of a fine Vietnamese cook and a maid. He managed the Embassy administratively. As Political Officer, I served as the Ambassador's alter ego.

We had no air-conditioning in the house. Energy was a serious problem in Vientiane. The country had neither oil nor coal, and had not yet developed water power. Electricity was generated by burning charcoal and the voltage was so low that you could not read by lamplight. At the office we did have window air-conditioners, run by portable gasoline-powered generators.

While living conditions were somewhat primitive and there was little entertainment, my job proved to be fascinating. In Rome I was dealing with a middle-level official in the Ministry of Foreign Trade. Here I frequently dealt with the Foreign Minister and, in the absence of the Ambassador, with the Prime Minister. I got to know every significant politician in Laos. Three of the most important were Nhouy (Abhay), Phoui (Sananikone), and Bong (Souvannivong). I have put their surnames in parentheses because everyone in Laos was known by his first name. There were so many Sananikones in Laos that it would have been confusing to use the surnames. Often I would stroll around in the evening, see them on their porches, and stop for a casual visit.

Another great boon was working with Charles Yost, our Ambassador and Chief of Mission. He exemplified the finest in the traditional Foreign Service. Son of a well-to-do family in northern New York State, he had gone to the Hotchkiss School, Princeton, and the University of Paris. Entering the Foreign Service in 1930, he served in Alexandria and Warsaw, where he met and married a beautiful Polish girl. To do so, he resigned from the Foreign Service in 1933 and worked as a free-lance journalist until he was hired by the Department of State in 1935. He rose through the ranks to become Ambassador to Laos, Syria, and Morocco. In 1961 Adlai Stevenson chose him as a Deputy Permanent Representative to the UN Security Council, a position he retained under Arthur Goldberg when the latter became our Permanent Representative after Stevenson died in 1965. In 1969, President Nixon appointed Yost as the U.S. Permanent Representative to the UN, the first career diplomat to hold that post. Replaced in that post by George Bush (later President), Yost became a distinguished lecturer at Columbia University and president of the National Committee on U.S.–China Affairs. He also wrote three brilliant books on foreign affairs: *The Age of Triumph and Frustration, The Insecurity of Nations*, and *The Conduct and Misconduct of Foreign Affairs.*

Of medium height and very slender, Yost was soft-spoken, modest, and unassuming in manner. But he was a man of great courage and decisiveness, who did not hesitate to speak his mind, gently but firmly. His views would often prevail because of the clarity of his thinking, his mastery of the subject matter, and his eloquence in expressing them. I could not have asked for a better model and teacher.

For most of my stay in Laos, the Prime Minister was Prince Souvanna Phouma, member of a cadet branch of the royal family. (Laos was then a kingdom.) His half brother, Prince Souphannavong, was leader of a rebel group supported by North Vietnam and bent on Souvanna's overthrow. They were both trained engineers, and I believe the only ones in the country. Supposedly, the revolutionaries were communists, even though Laos, having no real industry, had no proletariat. In any case, they were supported by the communists in North Vietnam.

Fighting was going on in the area close to Vietnam, but not in Vientiane itself. Under the Geneva agreements, no outside military were to be brought in, yet the United States wanted to help the royal government stay in power. So the United States provided training, military equipment, and funds for the Lao Army. We could not provide the will to fight, and that proved to be a fatal weakness.

The military officers who came to oversee the training and use of equipment were in mufti, so as not to violate the Geneva Agreement. They were called Program Evaluation Officers. Inspired by the fact that there was a mountain tribe in Laos called Meo, we dubbed them PEO. They were nice men who did their job quietly and unobtrusively.

We also had an economic aid mission, which was in charge of using the dollars exchanged for the Lao Kip (the local currency) that paid for Lao army costs. Much of those dollars were used to buy consumer items from the West in order to combat potential inflation resulting from the excess

Kip (local currency) in circulation. I disagreed with that policy on the grounds that there were relatively few Lao who could afford to buy the imported items. Indeed, many of the goods authorized for import never came in; they were diverted for sale in Hong Kong or Bangkok, with the proceeds going to Chinese merchants in Laos and payoffs to corrupt Lao politicians. I felt that the funds should have been used as capital for development to meet the future needs of Laos.

In the summer of 1955, there was widespread famine in Laos because of inadequate rain. It was decided that Alex Moore, an AID officer, and I should take a field trip to estimate the need. The plan was to leave early in the morning by Land Rover on a trip to Savannaket in Southern Laos. We were accompanied by Lao officials, who unfortunately showed up two hours late. As a result we were unable to make it to Savannaket and had to spend the night in a hill village in between. The headman of the local village treated his unexpected guests with generous hospitality. The villagers killed and barbecued several chickens to feed us. These chickens were tough. They were not fed; they had to scrounge around with the dogs and pigs to find their food, and thus became quite muscular. My jaws actually hurt from chewing the tough meat.

After dinner we went to sleep in the headman's bamboo house. We stretched out next to each other, Lao and Americans, on straw mats. A Lao stretched out next to me called, "Quinine, quinine." I guessed he had malaria, but I had no quinine, nor did I know the Lao language enough to say so. For want of any better response, I handed him two aspirins, which, I hope, gave him temporary relief.

The next day we made our way to Savannaket and many villages to the west of it. We saw plenty of evidence of famine—painfully thin adults and children with distended bellies. When we returned to Vientiane we made a strong recommendation that rice be provided.

Doing so was not easy. Washington was prepared to send 5,000 tons of American rice, but Thailand objected on the grounds that Laos was their traditional market. The United States pointed out that there was no market—the people involved were too poor to pay—but this did not mollify the Thai. Finally, an agreement was reached; the United States would deliver 5,000 tons of rice to Japan, which would buy a like quantity of Thai rice for delivery to Laos. This not only mollified the Thai; it also provided glutinous (sticky) rice to the Lao, who were accustomed to that type. It also suited their habit of eating with their fingers rather than implements.

In the process I learned something about logistics. Under the agreement the party with the lesser transport costs would reimburse the other for the difference. It turned out that it cost more to deliver Thai rice to neighboring Laos than American rice from New Orleans to Yokahama. In the latter case the rice was loaded and unloaded by machine, with a sea voyage in between.

The Thai rice had to be carried by ox cart to a railhead, loaded on a freight car, unloaded at the Makong River to be put on a ferry, then carried by truck to the distribution point. Then the bags were dropped by plane to the various famine areas. From time to time we had congressional visitors who wanted a "firsthand look" at the country. For the most part they stayed briefly in Vientiane, usually a matter of hours, and then left after a briefing by Embassy staff. An exception was Mike Mansfield, Majority Leader of the Senate. He came with his seasoned assistant, Frank Valeo, and really took time to look around. He had a scratchy personality and was really put off by anyone who tried to play up to him by flattery or obsequiousness. I drew the assignment to escort him to Luang Prabang, the royal capital. We flew up north in the Army attaché's plane, and I sat in the front row reading while the Senator and Valeo were in the row behind. About halfway through the flight Mansfield came to sit next to me and we had a good talk about the country, its people, and its problems. Mansfield loved Luang Prabang, which was in the Northern mountains and still unspoiled. It reminded him of the remote mountain areas of his home state, Montana.

Another senator, Everett Dirksen, decided not to come to Laos but instead to be briefed about the country in Bangkok. I flew down to do the briefing. I was prepared not to like Dirksen because I disagreed with his position on many issues and he appeared pompous on television. To my surprise he turned out to be a pleasant, gracious, and considerate host. I briefed him aboard a small riverboat where we had breakfast and it was a very enjoyable experience.

Another flight to Bangkok was not so pleasant. I contracted amebic dysentry in Loas, where I could not get adequate treatment. I flew down on a Saturday morning via Air Laos (a DC-3) and went to the Seventh Day Adventist Hospital in Bangkok for diagnosis and treatment. They prescribed and gave me aureomycin pills, to be taken every six hours around the clock. This meant getting up at 2 A.M., eating a sandwich, and drinking a glass of milk before taking the pill. I flew back to Vientiane Monday morning and went to work. We were between ambassadors, the Lao politicians were visiting Beijing, and there was a lot of work to do for Wendell and me.

Fortunately the pills worked. In three days my symptoms disappeared though, on instructions, I continued taking them for three weeks. I never had a recurrence, but on my return to the United States had to have a proctoscope every six months for several years to make sure there was no damage to the colon. The Foreign Service is not without its health hazards!

CHAPTER VII

Life in the Big Time: Henry Cabot Lodge and the United Nations

Having had five posts overseas, I expected my next assignment to be at the State Department in Washington. To my surprise there came a telegram assigning me to the U.S. Mission to the United Nations. I had no idea that Foreign Service people were assigned there.

Arriving in the United States, I had another surprise. I was told in Washington that the Permanent Representative, Henry Cabot Lodge, wanted to see me in New York before making a final decision on my assignment. This was, as far as I know, unprecedented in the Foreign Service, which usually makes unchallenged assignments. But Lodge was no ordinary Ambassador. He had gone to Paris to persuade Eisenhower to run for President and was very active in Eisenhower's campaign. After the election he represented Eisenhower during the transitional period in all parts of the government except the Treasury. He remained very close to the President and served in the Cabinet in addition to being our Permanent Representative to the UN. He had earned the privilege of selecting his staff. In any case, our interview went well and my assignment as Senior Economic Advisor was confirmed.

Eisenhower had made it clear that he wanted Lodge's advice not just on UN matters but also on "politics generally." Eisenhower said he would ask for advice but urged that Lodge should not wait to be asked. In eight years the President wrote Lodge about 150 letters, who in turn wrote a much larger number to Eisenhower. And there was a great deal more oral and informal communication, by telephone and in many Lodge visits to Washington.[1] Moreover, Eisenhower appointed Maxwell Rabb as cabinet staff secretary; Rabb had been Senator Lodge's administrative assistant, and this appointment gave Lodge an additional pipeline into the policy-making process.

Lodge's closeness to Eisenhower was further underlined by his appointment as special adviser to the President on November 15, 1953. In this capacity he counseled the President on many domestic political issues: he urged Eisenhower to lead public opinion, using television; to be the advocate of "modern Republicanism" and against reactionaries; not to attempt a purge of Republican mavericks in the 1954 congressional elections; to reject Senator McCarthy's smears against veteran Foreign Service professionals like John Service, John Carter Vincent, and Charles E. Bohlen; and to have presentations of policy made by an expert on Congress rather than someone expert only on the issue. Although Eisenhower's degree of success on these issues varied, there is no doubt that this "extracurricular" role strengthened Lodge's relationship with the President and thus added to his influence in making policy for the U.S. role in the United Nations.

In answer to questions I asked him, Lodge, on October 21, 1977, wrote the following about his relationship with Eisenhower:

I think in an average year I would breakfast with him twice a month and when Secretary Dulles was so seriously ill at the time of the Suez incident in '56, I was talking frequently with him on the telephone . . .

I knew President Eisenhower so well that I could pretty well anticipate what he would think about a given subject. Of course, we always had instructions whenever there was time to draft them. But, as you know, a member will suddenly make a motion in the middle of the voting and the U.S. Representative has to meet the issue then and there. He must either vote "yes" or "no" or abstain. Under those circumstances there is not even time to make a telephone call. But Washington never had to repudiate any decision that I took because I was so familiar with the thinking in Washington."

Eisenhower told Lodge that he wanted the American case to be presented "with life, cleverness, and effectiveness" at the UN,[2] and my observation of Lodge during four years together was that he did so with extraordinary skill. He was a highly effective speaker with a great sense of timing and an unusual ability to find the pungent phrase. He answered every Soviet attack with an immediate rebuttal. His own major addresses to the UN General Assembly were usually given just before noon, in time to catch the evening television news and the next morning's newspaper.

Eisenhower stressed that importance be attached to the UN, and building public support for it. Lodge did this so well that opinion surveys showed American support for the UN rising from 55 percent in 1953, when he arrived at the UN, to 80 percent in 1960 when he left.[3]

In addition to his closeness to the President and his well-developed media sense, Lodge had other significant assets. He was the scion of a distinguished Massachusetts family and was very proud of it. Though he had been a Senator and a Major General and had the title of Ambassador at the UN, he chose to be called "Mr. Lodge"—or "Cabot" if you got to know him well. He was patrician in bearing and took great care to greet staff members, receptionists, and security guards in a friendly manner.

Though not an intellectual like Stevenson, Lodge was a first-rate executive. He reached decisions quickly and slept well afterward. He did not hesitate to take responsibility or assume leadership or to get criticisms off his chest when he thought someone on his staff or in Washington had erred or failed to do his job. Moreover, he picked his staff with great care and was keenly aware of how each person was performing. He liked people who would stand up to him and argue vigorously against his viewpoint.

For his deputy, Lodge picked an old friend, James J. ("Jerry") Wadsworth, who served with him for all his eight-year tenure and succeeded to the job of permanent representative in the latter part of 1960 when Lodge resigned to run for vice-president. (Eisenhower in 1953 had suggested Ralph Bunche, a highly regarded black assistant secretary general at the United Nations and a Democrat, as deputy, but Bunche declined.)[4] Lodge tended to entrust Wadsworth with responsibility in particular areas, notably arms control, rather than use him as an overall operating executive. In fact, Lodge was his own operating executive, ably assisted by the minister counselor, James Barco, a highly capable, intelligent, and tireless worker who ran the staff on a day-to-day basis. Barco, a relatively young man, was elevated to the minister counselor job because Lodge felt that men of his ability should be moved up fast in order to serve to their full capacities. For similar reasons Lodge promoted Charles Cook, a young man who had been appointed to USUN's staff by Warren Austin upon graduation from Columbia Law School in 1950, as deputy counselor. He and Barco make the counselor's office the nerve center of the mission, serving as right-hand men to Lodge.

Except for Wadsworth and part-timers like Mason Sears, representative to the Trusteeship Council, and John C. Baker, representative to the Economic and Social Council, Lodge's staff was characterized by youth, ability, extraordinary diligence, virtual anonymity, and by no evident political party affiliation. Although I had an excellent working relationship with Lodge—in 1963, when he was ambassador to South Vietnam, he asked me to come out as his deputy, and in 1980 he wrote the foreword for my book, *Your Man at the UN*—he did not know until I told him in 1974 that I often voted for Democrats. The nonpartisan viewpoint at USUN was continued by Adlai Stevenson, who retained most of the same staff, except for the top five posts.

Only about 10 percent of the staff—three out of approximately 30 professionals—were career Foreign Service officers (FSOs) who had served elsewhere, as had also been the case under Austin. USUN was not an attractive post for FSOs. Living costs were very high; there were no rent allowances; entertainment funds were pitifully small; the twelve-hour day was normal; and an FSO was removed from the geographic bureaus that controlled future assignments. In recent years rent allowances have been provided, and the State Department has made it a matter of policy to fill most substantive posts with FSOs. Also, salaries have been raised substantially.

Lodge's main interest in my area was in the extent to which we could use economic policies to enhance our political position at the UN. In a sense we were in competition with the Soviets in a struggle to win the good will of the Third World countries, most of them underdeveloped. Later they were referred to as "less developed" and then, euphemistically as "developing."

In particular, Lodge was concerned that our opposition to SUNFED (Special UN Fund for Economic Development) was costing us support from the Third World. Yet there was no way that the U.S. Treasury or Congress would support SUNFED, which appeared to be a program for which the United States would put up most of the money and everybody else would decide how to spend it.

Lodge felt strongly that the United States would lose ground to the Soviets if we did not respond more sympathetically to the SUNFED drive. (The Soviets had declared in various UN forums that they would contribute to SUNFED if all other major contributors did.) Accordingly, on May 11, 1956, he wrote Eisenhower a letter proposing "UN Multilateral" under which the United States would earmark the $75 million per year then going into bilateral aid for a multilateral fund provided that other countries would match U.S. contributions so that this would constitute about one-sixth of the total. Also built in would be a provision that no allocations would occur except with the approval of the World Bank.[5] Lodge's proposal was rejected in Washington, following strong opposition by George Humphrey, the powerful Secretary of the Treasury.

When I came to USUN as economic adviser in September 1956, one of the first things Lodge discussed with me was his desire "to get this monkey off our backs." He asked whether we could work out a "Baby SUNFED" of about $100 million, with the United States contributing up to one-third, that would be welcomed by the less developed countries (LDCs) and could gain acceptance in Washington. We then became involved in a hectic General Assembly, on which were overlaid emergency sessions to consider the Suez and Hungarian crises; hence, there was no opportunity to move ahead until 1957. Meanwhile, Paul G. Hoffman, a progressive Republican who had been administrator of the Marshall Plan and a strong advocate of economic aid, served as our delegate to the Second (Economic) Committee of the General Assembly. Because of Paul's interest and reputation, we had unusual opportunities to consult during the session with the most active leaders of delegations to the Second Committee as well as with knowledgeable Secretariat officials. A series of working lunches with the Canadian delegation was particularly useful. Although a majority of more than three-quarters could have been mustered easily to establish SUNFED, its advocates wisely refrained from pressing the issue to a vote. Still, Hoffman and I advised Lodge in December 1956 that the LDCs were no longer interested in the 1953 Eisenhower promise and that, if general and complete disarmament could be achieved, the United States would consider devoting a part of the resources saved to programs toward the development of poorer countries. Disarmament was elusive and their needs were pressing.

The first half of 1957 was devoted to a search for a new formula, in consultations involving USUN and the State and Treasury Departments. Early on I advised Lodge that a Baby SUNFED would not work. With some 100 countries and territories to be aided, $100 million would average out to $1 million each. Not many bridges or harbors could be built for that sum—putting a second level on the George Washington Bridge cost $185 million! Embarking on a Baby SUNFED would mean either that the contribution to development would be trivial or that the capital to be provided would have to be many times the amount envisaged.

Our answer was a program originally called the Special Projects Fund. This new fund, plus the existing Expanded Program of Technical Assistance (EPTA), would have a joint target of $100 million, with the United States contributing up to 40 percent. It would not finance capital projects; rather, it would provide "preinvestment" assistance—resource surveys and the building of training institutions in LDCs, thus laying the groundwork for more and more effective capital investment, public and private, domestic and foreign.[6] Lodge put his full weight behind the proposal, and it was approved by Washington in time for the twelfth session of the General Assembly in September 1957.

The U.S. delegate to the Second Committee in 1957, Congressman Walter Judd, was a very different Republican from Paul Hoffman. An ardent supporter of Chiang Kai-shek, Judd told us shortly after he came to New York that, far from supporting the new Special Projects Fund, he believed that the existing EPTA should be abolished, with U.S. funds for multilateral technical assistance going directly to each specialized agency instead of being channeled through EPTA.

We did not argue with Judd but instead exposed him at small lunches and meetings to key representatives of LDCs and the more liberal developed countries (Canada, the Netherlands, and the Scandanavian countries). Gradually they changed his viewpoint. By December, Judd had not only fought hard for the Special Fund, he had become extremely popular with the LDCs, even with the Indians, Egyptians, and others who held views diametrically opposed to his on Chinese representation. His zeal, fervor, and honesty were appreciated, particularly after he changed his views on UN economic programs.

Judd helped greatly in achieving the compromise embodied in General Assembly resolution 1219 (XII), which provided for establishment of the Special Fund. It was largely worked out in backroom negotiations involving about a dozen delegations (not including the Soviet bloc), who then sold it to the rest. The United States promised it would stick to the agreement against any objections of recalcitrant developed countries, and the LDCs promised to do likewise with their recalcitrants; otherwise, no agreement would have been possible.

During the first days of negotiations we received instructions from Washington that we should attempt to delete the word "projects" from the title "Special Projects Fund," because the Treasury Department was afraid that it implied capital financing. Almost simultaneously, representatives of the LDCs proposed its deletion because they were afraid it would imply that the new program could never go into such financing. The U.S. delegation was thus in the happy position of being able to acquiesce gracefully to the LDC request for deletion.

The agreement on the text of resolution 1219 was reached in a backroom negotiation at about 10:30 P.M. on December 10, subject to our obtaining clearance from Washington on a statement concerning the U.S. contribution. Walter Judd phoned Washington for approval and was told by John Hanes, Jr., then Deputy Assistant Secretary of State, that "Congress wouldn't take that language." At that point, Judd exploded: "Hell, I'm a Congressman; I ought to know what they'll take!" That settled it.

During Second Committee consideration of resolution 1219, Judd pledged his best efforts with Congress to stabilize the U.S. contribution to the Special Fund and EPTA at 40 percent, then the level of our contributions to the EPTA program of $30 million. (Events proved he was a better judge of his congressional colleagues than Hanes.) This statement, an important factor in the successful negotiations, was remarkable for two reasons: (1) a few months earlier Congress had adopted a bill under which the U.S. contribution ceiling for EPTA would go down to 33 ⅓ percent; (2) Judd had arrived in New York three months earlier with serious doubts as to whether EPTA should be continued at all and with no commitment to the Special Fund. His contacts with Lodge, a fellow Republican, and with many other delegates from around the world changed Judd's mind, and he was all the more effective with Congress because of his record of staunch conservatism. From the UN standpoint, it was an excellent example of the potential value of exposing Congressmen to the General Assembly and other delegates for three months.

Hoffman and Judd were both "Public Members" of the delegation. The U.S. delegation to each General Assembly consists of five delegates and five alternate delegates. The Permanent Representative is always the chief delegate and several members on his staff serve as either delegates or alternates. Many public members have been prominent Americans from various walks of life, e.g., Dr. Walter Mayo, George Meany, William Rogers, Henry Ford II, Paul Hoffman, Irene Dunne, Shirley Temple, and Pearl Bailey. Each year there are two members of Congress, from the House of Representatives in odd years and the Senate in even.

These public members are backstopped and guided by the Mission staff, who draft statements for them and sit behind them at meetings to provide guidance. With one minor exception the relationship between delegates and advisers was excellent during my fifteen sessions at the General Assembly.

The quickest studies were the members of Congress, who were used to making statements, getting staff advice, and working in a parliamentary situation. While working at the UN, the Congressmen and Senators were under instruction from the President and the State Department. They were not allowed to express viewpoints that differed from those instructions. Senator Frank Church, when he served on the delegation, refused to participate in UN discussion on Vietnam, since his position on that issue differed markedly from the Administration's.

The Soviets, for their own reasons, had denounced the Special Fund proposal from the outset, arguing that it would spell the death of SUNFED. Some of the LDCs also feared such a result and, they told us, had asked whether the Soviets would agree to contribute $25 million to SUNFED reqardless of what the United States did. When the Soviets refused, the LDCs felt they had no practical alternative to the U.S. proposal, especially since it did not actually close the door on SUNFED. Agreement was also helped greatly by Denmark and the Netherlands, both of which had supported SUNFED for years and were now urging the LDCs to accept the U.S. idea.[7]

In the General Assembly all delegations except the Soviet bloc, which abstained, supported resolution 1219. Subsequently, when the program was established in 1959 the Soviets joined in, but their annual contributions were meager and they had lost their credibility as friends of the LDCs on UN economic issues.

During negotiations, I had pointed out that the term "SUNFED" had negative connotations in the United States, where it was often described as a plan whereby we would put up most of the money and everybody else would decide how to spend it. As we groped for a term that would distinguish the Special Fund we had agreed on from the kind of fund still desired by the LDCs, I suggested, as a means of getting over a temporary negotiating roadblock, the term "UN Capital Development Fund," and it stuck. Indeed, in 1960 the General Assembly voted in principle to establish the UNCDF and in 1965 it was established; however, it has never received sufficient contributions to make it meaningful. Significantly, countries like Saudi Arabia, Iran, Iraq, and Kuwait, which were strong SUNFED advocates, did not see fit to make substantial contributions to UNCDF from the tens of billions of additional dollars they earned through the twelvefold increase of oil prices.

Yet the principle of multilateral soft loans did not die; it was incarnated in the International Development Association (IDA), established as an affiliate of the World Bank in 1959. IDA extends credit for up to 50 years at 1 to 2 percent interest, with an initial ten-year grace period during which there is no repayment. This is just the kind of capital assistance the LDCs had been demanding. The difference is that IDA comes under World Bank management and its weighted voting procedures. Where billions of dollars are involved, as they have been under IDA, it is almost inconceivable that the U.S. Congress and other parliamentary bodies would have voted the money for a fund under the ultimate control of the one-country, one-vote UN General Assembly. So, in my view, the establishment of IDA has been a great boon to the people in the LDCs.

In any case, the decision to establish the Special Fund, with the Soviets isolated, accomplished Lodge's political purpose; besides, it was economically sound and genuinely helpful to the LDCs. In his report to the President on December 19, 1957, Lodge listed it among the four major accomplishments of the twelfth session of the General Assembly.

When the Special Fund was established in January 1957, its eighteen-member Governing Council (half major contributors and half others) was to decide on a managing director on the recommendation of the Secretary General. Because the United States would be contributing 40 percent, it was assumed that the job would go to an American. The official U.S. candidate was John Davies, who had earlier tried unsuccessfully to be elected director general of the Food and Agriculture Organization (FAO), but there was also a Danish candidate—Paul G. Hoffman. The Danish representative, Nonnie Wright, was lobbying hard for Hoffman, who was also very popular among the LDCs; he had headed the Marshall Plan, represented the United States in the Second Committee at the 1956 General Assembly, and had written in February 1957 a *New York Times* magazine article advocating a massive increase in aid, including a new experimental fund of $100 million to conduct resource surveys.

How did Hoffman become the "Danish" candidate? While he served as a delegate in 1956, he invited foreign colleagues from the Second Committee to a lunch at the Century Club. Nonnie Wright, a woman who represented Denmark, was denied admission because of the Club's policy at that time. Hoffman, mortified, invited Nonnie and her husband to dinner, and they became good friends.

As this broad support for Hoffman became evident, I urged Lodge to ask for new instructions. Since he was interested in political impact, I told him that we would in all likelihood win more political points with Paul Hoffman at the head of a $15 million Special Fund than with a relative unknown and $50 million. Lodge agreed and we next talked to Hoffman to find out whether a man who had administered a Marshall Plan running at $4 *billion* per year would accept the direction of a program that in its first year might amount to only $15 million (because of the provision that the U.S. contribution could not exceed 40 percent). Hoffman's reply: "I'd take it if it were fifteen cents; it's the principle that counts." Our instructions were changed; Hoffman was approved and he remained for more than a decade. When the Special Fund and the EPTA were merged as the UN Development Program in 1965, Hoffman became administrator (chief executive) of the larger program. In no small measure it was due to Hoffman's superb advocacy (I never met a better salesman), his total dedication, and his standing with high government leaders in Europe and the United States that annual contributions rose from $38 million in 1959 to $269 million in 1972. Hoffman was 80 when he retired in 1972. The program, currently the largest technical assistance fund in the world, now runs at about $2 billion per year.

THE "MALAYAN RESOLUTION"

Conscious of the political and propaganda success of the Special Fund, in early 1958 I sought another idea that would have intrinsic merit and also give the West a political and propaganda advantage. I drafted a resolution designed to encourage foreign private investment by asking the UN secretary general to (1) find out from the governments of less developed countries in what sectors of their economic development they would want foreign private investment and under what conditions; and (2) inquire of potential major investors in industrialized countries what sectors would most interest them and under what conditions.

Next I showed the draft to Henry Bloch, chief of the Finance Division in the UN Secretariat, who would be the principal action officer if the resolution were approved. Experience had demonstrated that Secretariat reaction to a draft resolution had a significant influence on delegation attitudes toward it as well as on its implementation. Bloch made a number of most helpful suggestions, which were incorporated in the draft. The revised draft was cleared by Lodge and the State Department without significant change.

Next there came the tactical question of sponsorship. Overt U.S. sponsorship would diminish chances of success. After a few weeks of getting acquainted with the new delegates, I found an ideal sponsor—Mohammed Sopiee, head of the Malayan delegation to the Second Committee. Sophiee saw considerable merit in the proposal and also thought that his identification with it would help him at home. He was a moderate socialist and wanted to make it clear in Malaya that he was not a doctrinaire opponent of private enterprise.

Sopiee assembled a group of cosponsors from around the world (Argentina, Australia, Canada, Denmark, Japan, Laos, Liberia, Nepal, New Zealand, Pakistan, Peru, Philippines, Sudan, and Thailand) for what came to be known as the "Malayan resolution"—General Assembly resolution 1318 (XIII). It was supported by all except the communist delegations, with the Yugoslavs exercising a benign neutrality while the Soviets thundered vainly against it.

Secretary General Dag Hammarskjold was highly pleased because he realized how important it was for the UN to have the confidence of significant private interests in the United States and other industrialized countries. Moreover, since the needs of the less developed countries for capital and technology far exceeded what could be made available by governments, it was important to facilitate foreign private investments under mutually acceptable conditions. The process initiated by the Malayan resolution continued for more than a decade and resulted in many face-to-face meetings between government officials of the less developed countries and top industrialists and investment bankers from the developed countries. From the U.S. standpoint, it was also a political and propaganda plus, building links with Third World countries.

In fact, the key to better relations with the Third World representatives in the economic area was always a focus on their problems rather than an overt cold war approach, which turned them off. This was sometimes difficult for outsiders to understand. In 1958, when the late George Meany was U.S. delegate to the Second Committee, I drafted a general debate statement for him, emphasizing the problems of development and the American approach to them. I gave the draft to his political adviser, Jay Lovestone, who had at one time been a high official in the Communist Party of the United States and had, in disillusionment, become vehemently anti-Communist. Lovestone returned the draft with the comment: "But you didn't attack the Russians." I replied, "The great majority in this committee don't care about our quarrel with the Russians. They're interested in development." He said Meany would not give the speech unless there was an attack on the Russians. I added a paragraph about the great gap between the Soviet protestations of concern for the less developed countries and the meagerness of their aid. Meany made the speech and our friends in Second Committee simply ignored the anti-Soviet paragraph.

THE WORLD FOOD PROGRAM

In May 1960 Lodge called me to his office and said: "Max, the vice-president [Nixon] wants to do something about using food through the UN. Of course, he doesn't know anything about either one. Will you give me a short memo on it?"

Lodge's comment about Nixon, with whom he would run later in 1960, was typically candid. I felt that the idea of channeling food aid through the UN and using it as an element of development was good. It would help to feed some people who would otherwise go hungry, assist economic development marginally, and help strengthen the role of the UN. I had doubts about the ability of the UN to manage efficiently a mammoth operational exercise comparable to the existing bilateral American program. Consequently, I worked out the skeleton of a program under which the UN would serve as a "clearinghouse" where food aid agreements could be arranged, with detailed negotiations and operations to be worked out by the countries concerned. Lodge handed the memo to Eisenhower, and it was then processed through channels to become a U.S. initiative at the 1960 General Assembly.

At the Assembly we prepared the ground carefully, recruiting an appropriate group of cosponsors. The aim in getting cosponsors was to assemble a group large enough to have influence in all the various geographic blocs except the Soviet, yet not so large as to be unwieldy in dealing with amendments. We also had to work out problems with food-exporting countries such as Thailand, which wanted to be sure that food aid would not interfere with their markets.

In order to maximize the political and propaganda impact, the United States used a favorite Soviet device—asking for priority consideration of the item. In this instance the Soviet delegate, Georgi Arkadiev, actually increased the impact by opposing the priority request vigorously and repeatedly. At one point he tactlessly commented: "What is the hurry? People have been hungry for a long time." As a result, the item got maximum attention at the UN and in the media. The *New York Times* gave it front-page coverage for three consecutive days. The resultant resolution, General Assembly resolution 1496 (XV), October 27, 1960, was adopted unanimously. It requested the secretary general and the director general of the Food and Agriculture Organization (FAO) to prepare a report on the basis of which the next session of the General Assembly could take a decision on the establishment of a World Food Program.

In 1961 Orville Freeman became Secretary of Agriculture in the Kennedy administration. An able, energetic man, he succeeded in having the World Food Program established at FAO headquarters in Rome rather than at UN headquarters in New York. This defeated USUN's purpose of strengthening the UN politically by bringing the World Food Program under its aegis. It also placed policy responsibility in the Agriculture Department rather than in State, although the State Department would have input in the preparation of U.S. positions on the operation of the program.

The World Food Program has survived and grown, its essential soundness endorsed by a succession of American administrations. Like the Special Fund, it was thoroughly staffed out through all interested U.S. agencies before it became operational. The point is, however, that neither proposal is likely to have materialized if Lodge had not obtained a prior White House endorsement in principle. The problem for the bureaucracy then became not *whether* but *how*. Otherwise, the proposals would in all probability have died in a morass of bureaucratic infighting and inertia.

SUEZ, 1956

The eleventh session of the UN General Assembly was opened on November 12, 1956, instead of the usual September opening in substantial measure because Lodge had persuaded the Secretary General and other UN members that it would be unwise to have the Assembly in session during the U.S. elections.[8] Lodge was concerned about a number of sensitive issues, particularly the Arab-Israeli dispute. It is doubtful, however, that Lodge or anyone else in the top levels of American government knew how explosive the situation would become.

Provoked by continued fedayeen terrorist raids from bases in the Sinai Desert, Israel invaded Sinai on October 29, 1956, and advanced rapidly toward the Suez Canal. The next day Britain and France issued an ultimatum to Israel and Egypt calling for an end to fighting within twelve hours, the withdrawal of the forces of both sides to a distance of ten miles from each side of the Canal, and agreement by Egypt to allow Anglo-French forces to be stationed temporarily on the Canal for the purpose of separating the belligerents and insuring the safety of shipping. (Actually, the Israeli, British, and French actions had been planned secretly in advance.)[9] The ultimatum was rejected by Egypt, thus opening the way for the Anglo-French invasion that was to start with the bombing of Egyptian airfields and other military installations by British aricraft based on Cyprus.

Eisenhower's reaction was one of dismay. The United States had not been consulted by the British or French, nor even been informed in advance. He said: "We could not permit the Soviet Union to seize the leadership in the struggle against the use of force in the Middle East and thus win the confidence of the new independent nations of the world. But on the other hand, I by no means wanted the British and French to be branded as naked aggressors without provocation. After all, Nasser had unilaterally nationalized the Suez Canal, commercially and strategically important to France and Great Britain, our NATO allies."

Following Eisenhower-Dulles-Lodge consultations on October 29, the United States called for an immediate emergency meeting of the Security Council and introduced a draft resolution calling upon Israel to withdraw its forces from Egypt without delay and asking all member states to "refrain from the use of force or threat of force."[10] Britain and France vetoed this draft resolution, as well as a Soviet draft the same night.

With Dulles ill—he entered the hospital a few days later for an ileitis operation—Lodge and his USUN staff, particularly Barco, Cook, and Pedersen, were largely responsible for initiating policy suggestions and drafting statements in the fast-moving situation at the UN. At the same time, they were involved in frequent consultations with the Secretary General and his top deputies, Andrew Cordier and Ralph Bunche, along with other missions. As the Hungarian crisis broke out, while Suez alone would have involved more than full-time operation, the key people at USUN, other active missions, and the Secretariat were involved almost around the clock for weeks. USUN feared that the British and French might organize a challenge to the Assembly's right to consider the question. It prepared a legal brief upholding that right and lobbied extensively for it; however, there was no formal challenge, perhaps as a result of the broad support for the move following the British and French vetoes.

On November 1 the Security Council, at the initiative of the Yugoslav delegation, invoked the Uniting for Peace procedure and called an emergency session of the General Assembly. In the Assembly, on November 2, Dulles condemned the resort to force by Britain, France, and Israel, which could "scarcely be reconciled with the principles and purposes of the United States," which found support from a not particularly welcome source—the Soviet Union.

The two superpowers were able to agree on a compromise resolution sponsored by the United States, urging a cease-fire and a withdrawal of all forces behind the armistice lines. USUN lobbied extensively for the draft, securing solid Latin American support; it was adopted by a vote of 64 in favor, 5 opposed, and 6 abstentions. One of those abstaining was Lester Pearson of Canada, who claimed that the resolution had made "one great omission": it had not provided for a vital instrument to prevent another explosion in the Suez area—"a truly international peace and police force."[11] Even before Pearson spoke, there had been intensive consultations about such a force between USUN, Hammarskjold, Andrew Cordier, Ralph Bunche, and the Swedish, Norwegian, Yugoslav, and Canadian delegations. Hammarskjold was cautious and reserved at first, but then became convinced that this expansion of his authority was needed for the defense of Egypt and the principles of the UN Charter. Lodge also spent many hours with a skeptical Krishna Menon, who was finally persuaded to support the plan—an important factor, since India was then the leader of the nonaligned and had close relationships with Egypt and Yugoslavia. Subsequently, India and Yugoslavia provided a major part of the UN force in the Sinai. It was then decided that Pearson should be the official sponsor, and he introduced a draft resolution asking the Secretary General to submit within 48 hours a plan for the creation, "with the consent of the nations concerned," of an emergency international force "to secure and supervise the cessation of hostilities." The United States gave the plan its strong support, declaring that it was interested in a solution that would "meet the immediate crisis as well as something that would go to the causes and into the more long-range subjects."[12] The Soviet Union felt that coercive action would be preferable, but did not object strongly to the Canadian plan. Thus, the General Assembly, on November 3, approved the Canadian draft resolution by a vote of 57 to 0, with 19 abstentions. The abstainers included the Soviet bloc, Britain, France, Israel, Egypt, Australia, New Zealand, the Union of South Africa, Portugal, Austria, and Laos.

U.S. policy in the Suez crisis of 1956 has been sharply criticized because it alienated, at least temporarily, two important North Atlantic Treaty Organization (NATO) allies. In fact, former Secretary of State Dean Acheson believed that it came close to losing the United States its two closest allies, splitting the NATO alliance, and thus exposing western Europe to a communist takeover.[13] Yet, for practical as well as moral reasons, Eisenhower, Dulles, and Lodge saw eye to eye on the policy adopted. There was, first, a sense of outrage because the British and French had not bothered to consult their NATO ally on so important a matter as military action in the Middle East. Second, from a purely military standpoint, the punitive expedition seemed to be foundering and thus could not be presented to the General Assembly as a fait accompli. The United States, by supporting the Anglo-French venture or even by taking a neutral view of it, would have risked the ill will of a large majority of the UN membership and, in addition, would have been in an embarrassing position if the military action failed or bogged down. Most important, the United States feared the intervention of the Soviet Union in the Middle East through "volunteers" and the risk of sparking a major war through direct superpower confrontation in the contested area.

According to Lodge, Eisenhower believed that the Soviets were prepared to use force to bring about foreign withdrawal and, where expedient, to use the Soviet presence in the Middle East to seize oil resources or deny them to the West.[14] Accordingly, the president used his influence in persuading the British to back down. Once this decision was made, the UN "provided a convenient method whereby they [British and French] could extricate themselves with minimum embarrassment."[15]

While British and French disengagement was prompt, Israel was reluctant to withdraw in the absence of solid assurance of its security, including protection against terrorist raids from the Sinai. Eisenhower became impatient and asked: "Should a nation which attacks and occupies foreign territory in the face of United Nations disapproval be allowed to impose conditions on its own withdrawal?" But even Eisenhower noted that, contrary to his word, Nasser had sent Egyptian administrators back into the Gaza Strip after Israeli withdrawal. Finally, on March 1, 1957 Lodge affirmed at the UN "a U.S.-Israel understanding that Israeli withdrawal was linked to free passage through Aqaba, and that any armed interference would entitle Israel to rights of self-defense under the U.N. Charter."[16]

Nasser's proclaimed blockade of Aqaba in May 1967, in defiance of this understanding, triggered the Six-Day War in June 1967.

LODGE AND KHRUSHCHEV

In 1959 Soviet Chairman, Nikita Khrushchev, came to New York to participate in the UN General Assembly—the first time the top man in the Soviet Union came to the United States and the UN. TV news programs showed Khrushchev pounding the table in front of him with his shoe. I also witnessed him twice interrupting the British Prime Minister with shouts in Russian. Hardly diplomatic behavior.

At the end of his stay in New York, Khrushchev crossed the United States to California to begin his tour of our country, with Lodge as his escort. In Los Angeles, Mayor Sam Yorty made remarks that Khrushchev considered insulting. He asked Lodge whether there was something Eisenhower could do to remove and punish Yorty. Lodge informed him that, under our system, there was nothing the President could do, Khrushchev then observed: "Poor Mr. Eisenhower!"

He was further infuriated when he was denied permission to go to Disney World because it would involve going through security zones. (This was a form of reciprocity in response to Soviet travel restrictions.) He was so angry that he threatened to fly home across the Pacific, canceling a planned trip back across the United States.

To calm him down, Lodge proposed a rail trip to Santa Barbara, using a train with an open rear observation platform. When Khrushchev agreed, Lodge got in touch with retired millionaire friends from Boston, urging them to come out and applaud the Soviet chairman. When the train got to Santa Barbara and Khrushchev was greeted with applause, he turned to Lodge and said: "You see, the common people, they like me." At any rate he was sufficiently mollified to go ahead with the planned trip across the United States, which included a visit with Roswell Garst in Iowa, who talked to him about effective ways of growing corn. And he left the United States in a good mood, thanks to Lodge's ingenious ploy.

Early in 1960 Lodge resigned in order to run for vice president on a ticket headed by Richard Nixon. He confided to me that Nixon promised to put him in charge of international affairs and said he would want me to come to Washington to be in charge of all international economic affairs. During the campaign there was friction between Nixon and Lodge. A patrician, Lodge tended to look down on Nixon, who had scratched his way up from a middle class background through intensive hard work. Nixon, on his side, considered Lodge a lazy campaigner and resented the latter's afternoon naps.

Although I liked working with Lodge and the job he portrayed would have been fascinating, I had no regrets about the election results. In my mind there was no way Nixon would have put Lodge in charge of all international affairs, given Nixon's own intense interest in that area and the total lack of precedent for such an action. By extension, there was no way I could have had the job Lodge envisioned.

Meanwhile, another tempting opportunity came up. The State Department offered me a chance to study Russian intensively at Columbia University for a year, after which I would become the first Minister for Economic Affairs in Moscow. I was sorely tempted, since my experience in Budapest gave me a strong interest in the economics of the Soviet bloc. Moreover, if I went to Moscow as a Minister I might be in line for the ambassadorship there some years later—one of the few top embassies not reserved for political appointees.

My wife was adamantly opposed to being uprooted and was apprehensive about Moscow. David Wilken, a former Foreign Service Inspector who had spent some time inspecting our Moscow Embassy, reinforced her fears. He told us of the sense of isolation felt by the Embassy staff, cut off from normal contact with the Russian people, many of whom had been driven to drink. We argued over it for about two months, after which I reluctantly agreed to decline the offer. At this point I gave up all hope of ever becoming an ambassador, but I could not force the issue with my wife.

SUMMER IN GENEVA

Each summer the UN Economic and Social Council holds its main meeting at the Palais des Nations in Geneva. As senior Economic Adviser I was supposed to be part of our delegation, as I was in 1957.

The Economic and Social Council (ECOSOC) with only eighteen members, almost half of them from industrialized countries, was a much more orderly place than the General Assembly. Its principal concern was the coordination of the UN's economic and social programs with those of the specialized agencies, i.e., the Food and Agriculture Organization, the International Labor Organization, the World Health Organization, the World Bank, and the International Monetary Fund. To me it seemed like an eighteenth-century minuet compared to the hurly-burly of the Second (Economic) Committee of the General Assembly. Unfortunately, the Second Committee frequently ignored ECOSOC. Efforts were made to strengthen the role of ECOSOC by enlarging its membership, first to 27 and then to 54, but these enlargements made little difference to its standing.

LODGE AND HAMMARSKJÖLD

At the outset of their relationship, Hammarskjöld was unknown to Lodge, and initially they regarded each other with reserve and occasional irritation. These were accentuated by the Guatemala issue in 1953, when

Lodge successfully forestalled Security Council action on the complaint of the leftist Arbenz regime that the United States was aiding a coup against it, on the grounds that this was a regional issue to be dealt with in the Organization of American States. The Soviet motion for adoption of the agenda on June 25 was rejected by a vote of four in favor, five against, and two abstentions (Britain and France). By June 27 the Arbenz government had fallen and the issue was moot. Hammarskjöld felt that the Security Council should at least have considered the issue and was annoyed with Lodge.[17]

In August 1953 Hammarskjöld went to Lodge's home in Beverly, Massachusetts, for the weekend, accepting uneasily. He enjoyed himself so thoroughly in the Lodge family circle that he and Lodge developed a personal friendship that grew steadily, offsetting some official disagreements that arose later—for example, the U.S. intervention in Lebanon in 1958.

Relations were further improved after Hammarskjöld's mission to China in 1955 resulted in the release of fifteen American fliers and by Hammarskjöld's masterful handling of the Suez crisis in 1956–1957 and the Congo crisis in 1960.

On at least two occasions Lodge asked Hammarskjöld to talk to the Secretary of State. While Hammarskjöld was negotiating for the release of American fliers, Dulles was making condemnatory statements about the Chinese. In a phone call, Hammarskjöld persuaded the Secretary to use more restraint. Again in the fall of 1956, with Lodge's full agreement, the Secretary General phoned Dulles to explain why it was necessary to station a UN Emergency Force on Egyptian soil; Lodge himself had been unable to convince Dulles. Washington's growing confidence in Hammarskjöld, as well as Lodge's good relations with him, was certainly a factor in Eisenhower's decision to encourage UN responsibility for the Congo crisis in 1960.

It is sometimes assumed today that the United Nations of the 1950s was a docile place where the United States could command a majority by snapping its fingers. In fact, Lodge and his staff had to work hard to sell American policies, cultivate other delegations assiduously, and make judicious compromises. Initiatives in the peaceful use of nuclear energy and in the economic field were used to build support among the less developed countries for things the United States wanted; even then the less developed countries commanded three-fourths of the votes. As far back as March 1954 Gladwyn Jebb, the British permanent representative, observed: "The great days when we and the Americans largely ran the show was over. The era of the 'underdeveloped' countries was about to begin."[18] Of course, the task of the U.S. permanent representative is now far more difficult, as the Third World country membership in the UN has doubled since the early 1960s and has become better organized and more militant, but it would be an illusion to believe that American policies were automatically accepted in the 1950s. Even then, acceptance required hard work, sensitivity, judicious compromise, and occasional pressure.

At least one experienced observer, Ruth Russell, felt that the United States had worked too hard and expended too much influence in order to win votes on cold-war issues.[19]

NOTES

1. Henry Cabot Lodge, *As It Was: An Inside View of Politics in the 50's and 60's* (New York: Norton, 1976), pp. 46–47.
2. Alfred O. Hero, Jr., "The United States Public and the United Nations," in David A. Kay, *The Changing United Nations* (New York: Academy of Political Science, 1977), p. 19.
3. Lodge, *As It Was*, p. 56.
4. Ibid.
5. Many of these ideas had been incorporated in *A Forward Look*, a document prepared by the UN Secretariat looking toward the further development of the Expanded Program of Technical Assistance.
6. For an account of the negotiations from the Dutch and Canadian point of view, see John G. Hadwen and Johan Kaufmann, *How United Nations Decisions Are Made* (Leyden: A. W. Sijthoff, 1960).
7. Eisenhower, *Waging Peace* (Garden City, NY: Doubleday, 1965), p. 83.
8. In 1948 this problem was handled by the decision of the members to convene the Assembly at the regular time (second Tuesday in September) but in Paris presumably away from the pressures the media could have generated. In fact, in 1956 there were proposals circulating to take the General Assembly to the United Kingdom. (Blackpool was the suggested locale.) The general breakdown in U.S.-U.K. communications, alluded to later, kept this idea from taking hold. It is interesting to speculate on how much of what is hereafter described would have taken place if the UN General Assembly had been in session, in full regalia, in the United Kingdom at the time of the Suez and Hungarian affairs.
9. John G. Stoessinger, *Crusaders and Pragmatists: Movers of Modern American Foreign Policy* (New York: Norton, 1979), pp. 114–24.
10. Eisenhower, *Waging Peace*, p. 83.
11. UN Doc. S/3712, October 29, 1956.
12. UN General Assembly, *Official Records*, 563rd meeting, November 3, 1956, pp. 55–71.
13. Dean Acheson, *Power and Diplomacy* (Cambridge, Mass.: Harvard University Press, 1958), pp. 109–16.
14. Lodge, *As It Was*, pp. 93–99.
15. Robert Rhodes James, "International Crises, the Great Powers and the United Nations," *International Journal* (Spring 1970).
16. Eisenhower, *Waging Peace*, p. 188.
17. Arnold Beichman, *The "Other" State Department* (New York: Basic Books, 1967), pp. 111–12, based on conversations with Andrew Cordier, former Undersecretary General of the United Nations.

18. Hubert Myles Gladwyn Jebb, *The Memoirs of Lord Gladwyn* (New York: Weybright and Talley, 1972), p. 267.

19. Ruth B. Russell, *The United Nations and United States Security Policy* (Washington, DC: Brookings Institution, 1968), pp. 540–41.

CHAPTER VIII

Adlai Stevenson

When President Kennedy came into office, his appointee to the UN was another outstanding political figure, Adlai Stevenson. Stevenson had been a strong supporter of the UN since its founding; he was a member of the U.S. delegation to the San Francisco conference that adopted the UN charter in 1945. He was not only a brilliant intellectual but also a highly successful political figure. He had won the govenorship of Illinois in 1948 by the largest majority in history. True, he lost the presidential elections in 1952 and 1956, but he was running against a highly popular wartime hero, Dwight D. Eisenhower.

Kennedy's choosing a man of such stature and international reputation was taken as a sign of the importance the new President ascribed to the UN. Stevenson's first appearance in the Security Council, on February 1, 1961, was greeted by a spontaneous outburst of applause. He continued to be enormously popular with other delegations.

In fact, however, Stevenson was to have much less influence on American policy than his predecessor, Lodge, but few members of the UN perceived that in 1961.

The key factor is the relationship with the chief policy maker, the President, and the Kennedy-Stevenson relationship lacked the closeness, personal friendship, and mutual trust that characterized that of Eisenhower and Lodge. Whereas Lodge was important in Eisenhower's successful candidacy and never a rival for it, Stevenson had refused to remove himself firmly from consideration in the 1960 race and rejected endorsement feelers from the Kennedy campaign staff.[1] Kennedy was also annoyed when Stevenson delayed for a week before accepting the UN post.[2] Stevenson wanted to be Secretary of State, but Kennedy told him in late November that he had taken too many public positions on prickly political issues and would in consequence be too controversial for Congress. Given the margin of the election, Kennedy said that he needed most of all a secretary of state who could get along on Capitol Hill. Finally, with whatever misgivings, Stevenson accepted the job as permanent representative because he found public life more exciting than private law practice, and he had a deep interest in the UN, dating back to its establishment.[3]

Arthur Schlesinger's view of the Kennedy–Stevenson relationship appears to me so perceptive and nuanced that it warrants quotation:

Kennedy, who had an essential respect and liking for Stevenson, tried, when he thought of it, to make their relationship effective. He understood Stevenson's standing in the world and his influence on liberal opinion in the United States, admired his public presence and wit, valued his skills as diplomat and orator, and considered him, unlike most of the State Department, capable of original thought . . . Kennedy fully expected, moreover, that people (including some of his own loyalists who still had not forgiven Stevenson for Los Angeles in 1960) would try to make trouble between Adlai and himself, and generally shrugged off the tales helpfully repeated to him of petulance or discontent in New York. On the other hand, certain of Stevenson's idiosyncrasies did try him; and his own effect on Stevenson in face-to-face encounter was unfortunately to heighten those who tried him most. The relationship was of course harder for Stevenson. He was the older man, and in one way or another Kennedy had denied him his highest hopes. Though Stevenson greatly respected the President's intelligence and judgment, he never seemed wholly at ease on visits to the White House. He tended to freeze a little, much as he used to do in the fifties on television shows like *Meet the Press*, and, instead of the pungent, astute and beguiling man he characteristically was, he would seem stiff, even at times solemn and pedantic.[4]

Although Schlesinger's account shows that Stevenson had some influence in Washington, my own experience at USUN during the period 1956–1965 indicates that he did not have the clout with Kennedy that Lodge had with Eisenhower. Schlesinger refers elsewhere to his uncomfortable position as a "middleman" between Kennedy and Stevenson, "two men whom I so much admired but whose own rapport was perhaps less than perfect."[5]

Moreover, during Stevenson's tenure far more of the initiatives and initial speech drafts came from Washington.[6] Also, Stevenson hesitated to call the president unless it was absolutely essential.[7] On the other hand, Stevenson was completely at ease with the First Lady and thoroughly charmed by her. It was not a romantic relationship, but they obviously enjoyed each other's company. During her visits to New York she always stopped by his office for a visit. Indeed, as John B. Martin observed:

Stevenson was unusually attractive to women all his life, and they attracted him. The ones who became close to him—and many more who tried—were nearly all bright, pretty, and rich, and several of them had newspaper connections. They were, most of them, also strong-willed, as his mother and sister had been. Unlike some political leaders, such as John F. Kennedy, Stevenson did not separate his political or official life from his private life. Kennedy had two sets of friends; those he worked with in politics or government, and those he saw socially, and to a considerable extent they were different people. Stevenson was inclined to mingle the two. The women in his life, except for his wife, gave him political advice. His most private letters to women are likely to contain his frankest views on public men and public issues—he confided more fully in women than in men.[8]

I believe that if a poll had been taken of women college graduates, Stevenson would have won 90 percent of the ballots. His wit, his intelligence, his sensitivity, and his vulnerability appeared to constitute a major attraction.

Stevenson's relations with the Secretary of State were courteous and showed a degree of mutual respect, but there was an underlying tension between them. Stevenson had agreed to take the UN post after Dean Rusk had been nominated as Secretary of State; however, he had wanted the secretary's job and considered himself better qualified for it. He respected Rusk's intellect and industry but referred to him as "just a good technician" and too "wooden" at cabinet meetings. Rusk, on his side, had a high regard for Stevenson's performance at the UN, but more as an advocate than as a counsel, though he felt that Stevenson provided "a useful yeast and ferment." Rusk came to New York at the opening of each General Assembly for private talks with foreign ministers present there, as had become the custom, but he never spoke at the Assembly. Although both believed in containment, Stevenson was willing to go further in trying to end the cold war, and this caused some friction. Stevenson chafed at taking instructions from Rusk and in December 1961 tried to obtain a recognized channel to the White House; however, Rusk and Cleveland objected to this approach, and it was not very effective.[9]

Rusk was a prodigious worker. The joke around the State Department was that Rusk's idea of a vacation was to put on a sport shirt and come to work on Sunday.

THE STEVENSON TEAM—AND ITS LEADER

Stevenson brought in a top layer of aides of unusual competence and distinction. His main political adviser was Ambassador Charles W. Yost, deputy representative to the UN Security Council. Yost had worked with Stevenson in the preparatory and founding stages of the UN, and they had a high regard for each other. A career diplomat of the highest intelligence and integrity, Yost was the "professional's professional." He served as Stevenson's top adviser on political and security issues. Experienced, wise, and articulate, Yost drafted many of the key policy memoranda for Stevenson and was involved in all of them. Like most USUN personnel, he found the post a financial as well as a physical drain. In 1963, at Stevenson's suggestion, William Benton provided $3,000 to supplement Yost's salary. In the same year Kennedy asked Yost to become ambassador to Yugoslavia, a highly interesting and important post with much better pay and perquisites. But Stevenson asked Yost to stay with him, and he did, to Kennedy's surprise and irritation.[10]

As deputy permanent representative Stevenson chose Francis T. P. Plimpton, an old friend and former roommate at Harvard Law School and a liberal Republican. A highly successful lawyer and an intelligent gentleman, Plimpton was in general charge of the mission under Stevenson. He worked hard and effectively at his job and resented the use of the term "working level" to designate those below the rank of ambassador.

Plimpton also entertained foreign diplomats frequently and well, often using his country place on Long Island. Perhaps because of his wealth and distinguished family background, he could not seem to avoid a certain air of condescension toward Third World diplomats; even those he liked. On numerous occasions I heard him refer to the permanent representative of one foreign country or another as "that nice little fellow from ———." Stevenson, though of similar background, showed no condescension in his manner; however, when he wanted to relax and enjoy life he habitually did so with people of wealth and position. Frequently, too, he asked Plimpton to represent him at the numerous UN social functions that he found boring, a function Plimpton fulfilled conscientiously and well. With his tendency for humorous hyperbole, Stevenson told John B. Martin, "Francis is my oldest friend but he has all the political sex appeal of a dead mouse."[11]

The post of representative to the Economic and Social Council was given new importance by according its new incumbent, Philip M. Klutznick, the rank of ambassador. Klutznick, a dynamic, hard-driving, and highly intelligent lawyer, had make a fortune in real estate development in the Chicago area and had been a supporter of Stevenson's campaigns. Because of his experience, skills, and energy, he was given responsibility not only for economic and social affairs but also for the U.S. interest in the UN's budget and finance activities. He was the principal negotiator of the UN bond issue of 1961, which kept the Congo operation financially afloat. It is indicative of the political affairs bias of most writers in the field that I could find no account of his activities at the UN in existing books except brief references in John B. Martin's two-volume biography of Stevenson.

Klutznick, a lifetime Zionist, had written a book about the Middle East called *No Easy Answers*, then still in galley form. At Stevenson's request, I read the manuscript and wrote him a memorandum about it. In my view, substantial sections of it were so pro-Israel and anti-Arab as to constitute an embarrassment to an American official at the UN. Stevenson, instead of speaking to his friend, Klutznick, on the basis of my memorandum, asked me to meet with him. Since Klutznick was slated to become my new boss, the situation was ticklish. In any case, I gave him my views with complete frankness, seeing no decent alternative. His first reaction was explosive; he said he would rather not take the job than alter the book. On reflection, however, he changed his mind and did revise the manuscript. Interestingly, it was the beginning of an excellent working relationship and friendship between us. (It is ironic that Klutznick, who became president of the World Jewish Congress in 1978, has been criticized by many Israeli hard-liners for his friendly relations with Egypt's President Sadat and his identification in 1976 with a Brookings Institution panel that recommended a comprehensive Middle East settlement. In January 1979 he became the Secretary of Commerce.)

The job of U.S. representative to the UN Trusteeship Council was also raised to the ambassadorial level, made full-time, and given to Jonathan Bingham, a liberal Democrat. Two longtime personal friends, Marietta Tree, who frequently accompanied him on official and personal trips, and Jane Dick were named representatives to the Commissions on Human Rights and Social Development, respectively. The post of counselor of mission went to Charles Noyes, who had served at USUN under Warren Austin; his job was mainly coordination, because the high-powered top layer left no room for a counselor with the power and policy impact that James Barco had under Lodge.

Another important appointment was Eleanor Roosevelt, who served as a delegate to the General Assembly in 1961. Though she was then 77, her mind was still functioning beautifully. Her comments at delegation meetings were always wise and modestly advanced. As chair of the UN Commission on Human Rights, she was substantially responsible for the framing and adoption of the Universal Declaration of Human Rights in 1948. Her unassuming manner was manifested in many ways, including her use of the New York subway to travel from her home in Manhattan to the Commission's meeting place in the Bronx. On one occasion she apologized profusely for being late because of a delay in the subway!

She died in 1962 and, with others, I accompanied Stevenson to her funeral at Hyde Park. He delivered a beautiful eulogy, describing her as a woman who would rather light candles than curse the darkness. Three presidents came—Truman, Eisenhower, and Kennedy—a fitting tribute to this great lady.

At the staff level USUN was largely a carryover from Lodge. Richard Pedersen headed the political section; Albert Bender, the section dealing with the UN budget, personnel, and organization; and I, the economic and social section. Clayton Fritchey, a veteran of the newspaper and political worlds and a Stevenson friend since his service in the 1952 campaign, headed the public affairs section, but Frank Carpenter remained as press officer, as did most other personnel in the section.

It was a formidable array of talent but was not always as well managed and led as the staff had been under Lodge or was to be under Goldberg. The very existence of so many stars at the top, all with personal ties to Stevenson, made it more difficult to pull all parts of the staff together. Moreover, Stevenson was not a full-time mission chief. His prominence as a national and world political personality made enormous extracurricular demands on his time, such as correspondence, speaking engagements, meetings, and an important role in the Field and Eleanor Roosevelt Foundations. On top of all that, he led an extremely hectic social life even beyond the already exhausting official social activities involved in UN diplomacy.

Stevenson was plagued by indecisiveness. One biographer refers to him as "a bundle of unreconciled and unresolved contradictions."[12] Part of his difficulty in making up his mind on political issues arose from his excellent habit of looking at all sides of a problem rather than take a position prematurely. Yet another part of the problem was a degree of personal insecurity and self-doubt. I recall one delegation meeting at which we were trying to decide on a resolution about the Portuguese territories in Africa. A spokesman for the Bureau of European Affairs argued that we must vote against it to show our solidarity with Portugal, which was providing a military base for us in the Azores. The African affairs man said we must vote for the resolution to maintain good relations with the anti-Colonial African countries. My field then was economic affairs, but I asked the question: "Why don't we vote our own convictions?" Phil Klutznick, a longtime friend of Stevenson, told me that Adlai did not sleep all night. Apparently his conscience was disturbed by the fact that he had not taken the position I suggested. I cannot imagine that Lodge, Goldberg, Ball, or Bush would have been upset under similar circumstances.

One writer has attributed Stevenson's self-doubts to a hunting accident when he was seventeen; he accidentally shot and killed a cousin. Another problem was cited by Lord Caradon, the former British permanent representative and a man of wide experience and objectivity, who thought that Stevenson was too fastidious for the ferocity and dirtiness of international negotiations. I can recall cringing for Stevenson when the Soviet representative, the sarcastic Nikolai Fedorenko, would attack him personally while Stevenson was too much of a gentleman to respond. I hated Fedorenko for it. Arthur Goldberg, accustomed to the rough and tumble of labor politics, had no trouble dealing with Fedorenko. (Stevenson was temperamentally disinclined toward personal animosities, but there was one public figure he loathed and despised—Richard Nixon, whom he considered sly, slippery, and thoroughly unprincipled.)[13]

Also, because of his self-doubts, Stevenson did not fight hard and aggressively in Washington on policy issues. With a President attuned to decisive action, surrounded by self-assured, assertive advisers such as McGeorge Bundy, Robert McNamara, and Walt Rostow, Stevenson might weigh in on policy, but his influence was rarely decisive. As has been noted, he simply did not have the clout that Lodge had with Eisenhower or Goldberg had in his first year and a half with Johnson.[14]

According to Arthur Schlesinger, 70 percent of the problem was a function of simply not being in the room when policy was being made in Washington. Thirty percent was that even when he was in the room Stevenson was not quite putting a legitimate point in a framework that would relate to the machine of government. "Stevenson had against him the whole apparatus of the Department of State except for Harlan Cleveland intermittently."[15]

John B. Martin quotes Stevenson's longtime, close friend George Ball, as follows:

After the Cuban missile crisis [1962] Adlai was only going through the motions. His role had become ritualistic. From then on he knew he was not going to have an impact on foreign policy—which was what was most important to him. Washington was a force of its own and he was not part of it. He was a member of the Cabinet but not really. He'd call me up and say, "I can't change anybody's view. The President is being misled and getting bad advice." But he didn't think for a minute that anything he said was going to change anything. I loved Adlai but by the time he died I felt he was almost a caricature of himself—a hollow man.[16]

Martin then comments that Ball was "to some extent employing hyperbole. Stevenson probably realized much earlier, perhaps as early as the Bay of Pigs, that he would not exert decisive influence on much of policy. He continued to try, however. The defeatist mood that Ball was describing did not dominate until the last half year or so of his life." Yet there was, for example, a notable difference between Ball's forthright opposition to American involvement in Vietnam and Stevenson's soul-searching, hesitating doubts about the intervention.

Stevenson was also deeply disappointed at being shut out of disarmament negotiations by both Kennedy and Johnson. He had proposed a nuclear test ban treaty in 1956, the first major American politician to do so, yet he had no significant role in negotiating the partial test ban treaty endorsed by the UN General Assembly in 1963.[17]

But there was also a strong positive side. Stevenson did have standing in the world, public presence, wit, an original mind, and great skills as a diplomat and orator, all of which Kennedy appreciated. From my personal experience it was clear that Stevenson did not just read speeches drafted by others. Even in cases where he did not do the first draft, he went over a proposed statement with painstaking care, right up to the moment of delivery, often making eloquent what would have been humdrum. I was involved in one of the rare instances where he did not do extensive editing. We were at an Ecosoc meeting in Geneva, and he was away as a weekend guest of Gianni Agnelli. He arrived back only minutes before he was to speak; consequently, he had no time to revise the text. But his delivery gave it an eloquence it had not had before. I had done the final draft for him, in which I emphasized the fact that brains was the new growth industry. He spoke in 1961, and it turned out to be a prophetic statement.

He was also unusually decent and charming and had extraordinary energy. He genuinely believed in disarmament, the UN, relaxation of tension with the Soviets, and assisting the development efforts of the poorer countries as a way of building peace and stability. In crises at the UN, notably in the Cuban Missile Crisis and the Congo crisis, he displayed an iron nerve and performed superbly. He was highly popular among other delegates, including those of the Third World. Achkar Marof of Guinea expressed a widespread feeling when he commented: "When I heard he died my feelings were exactly as if World War III had broken out. He was so identified with peace, I thought, who's going to succeed him? Who's going to exercise a moderating influence?"[18] And Arthur Goldberg told several of us at USUN that he would not have considered leaving the Supreme Court if a man of Stevenson's stature had not been the permanent representative before him.

Moreover, Martin notes, "his words at the UN moved millions, advanced the American interest, and strengthened the United Nations. Indeed, herein may have lain his greatest contribution. He did not enlarge the role of U.S. Ambassador to the UN, because he could not. But he did play another role, and in the long run perhaps a more important one, that of unofficial UN Ambassador to the United States."[19] And Robert Kennedy said: "President Kennedy always thought he did a good job of keeping people happy at the UN. He did not make mistakes. He represented in an articulate way the United States in foreign eyes as well as could be. He was the best Ambassador we could have had there."[20]

THE CONGO

Stevenson's first test came within weeks of his arrival at USUN, with a resurgence of the Congo crisis. Patrice Lumumba, the former prime minister, had been placed under house arrest by General Mobutu, who led the coup in September 1960. In November Lumumba escaped from Leopoldville, where he had been under UN protection, to join his leftist supporters in Stanleyville, but was recaptured by Mobutu's troops four days later. In January 1961, Mobutu turned Lumumba over to the Katanga regime, and on February 13, Katanga radio announced that Lumumba had been killed in an attempted escape the day before. (A UN commission investigating the matter reported, on November 11, 1961, that Lumumba had in fact been executed.) In the meantime, Lumumba's lieutenant, Antoine Gizenga, had established a regime in Stanleyville that was recognized by the Soviet bloc and several of the more militant African states: the United Arab Republic, Ghana, Guinea, Mali, and Morocco.[21]

With civil war threatening, the Security Council met and on February 21 passed its strongest resolution to date, by a vote of 9 to 0, with France and the Soviet Union abstaining.[22] The prices paid to the various blocs among the UN membership were apparent in the provisions of the resolution— that Belgian and other military and paramilitary personnel be withdrawn, which was aimed directly at Tshombe's mercenaries; that the Congo parliament, in which Gizenga and the Lumumbist "radicals" could on most issues muster enough allies to command a majority, be convened; that the Congolese army be reorganized; and finally that the UN should take "all appropriate measures" to prevent the occurrence of civil war and that these appropriate measures should include not only arranging for cease-fires, the halting of military operations, and the prevention of clashes, but also "the use of force if necessary is the last resort."

In any case, Stevenson did not have to fight Washington on this issue, Kennedy, like Eisenhower, was convinced that "if we didn't have the UN operation, the only way to block Soviet domination in the Congo would be to go in with our own forces."[23] Stevenson himself told the Security Council, on February 15, 1961, that "the only way to keep the Cold War out of the Congo is to keep the UN in the Congo."[24] Strong support for this policy came not only from the President but also from the influential Assistant Secretary of State for African Affairs, Mennen Williams, and his deputy, Wayne Fredericks, as well as from Harlan Cleveland, the capable and supportive Assistant Secretary for International Organization Affairs, and Stevenson's old friend Undersecretary of State George Ball.[25]

Efforts to terminate the civil war by negotiations with the Katanga regime proved fruitless; its secession was finally ended through military action in 1963, the UN Force acting in "self-defense," on the grounds that the Katanga troops were interfering with its communications lines. Negotiations between Leopoldville and the Stanleyville regime in 1961 were, however, successful. Under UN aegis, the Congolese parliamentarians, meeting in accordance with the Security Council resolution of February 21, 1961, reached agreement. On August 1, they selected as premier Cyrille Adoula, a moderate like President Kasavubu who had been a friend of Patrice Lumumba's, although he had a different outlook. Antoine Gizenga, who had inherited Lumumba's mantle as leader of the leftist group in Stanleyville, was chosen as vice premier.[26] This parliamentary agreement was a brilliant success for UN "Good Offices."

After November 1961 there was little active consideration of the Congo in the Security Council, even though the operation continued for three more years.[27] As a result, the secretaries general, Hammarskjöld and U Thant, had to interpret existing instructions and work out procedures to deal with a situation that was always complex and often changed rapidly. That they remained true to the spirit of the resolution and the UN Charter, despite tremendous political pressures (e.g., Khrushchev's attack on Hammarskjöld in 1960 and his call on the Secretary General to resign), is a tribute to their integrity, impartiality, and political skills. Each kept abreast of the prevailing political currents at the UN, consulting the Congo Advisory Committee, composed of representatives of the countries contributing troops for the force, as well as a "Congo Club" of top Secretariat officials.[28]

The main axis of support for the Secretary General consisted of the United States, India, and key African states. As Lefever notes, "India and the United States were the two countries the UN operation most depended upon, both for political support in New York and for military support in the Congo." Despite some differences in interpreting the mandate, the United States–India partnership remained solid throughout the Congo drama. The Congo operation would probably have collapsed if either New Delhi or Washington had withdrawn its support before the infiltration of Katanga in January 1963.[29] This is particularly noteworthy, since India and the United States were so frequently at odds on other issues at the UN. India was the principal contributor of troops and military leadership during the crucial Katanga operation. The United States, like other major powers, did not contribute troops, but it was the mainstay for logistic, financial, and economic support. In New York, Stevenson met frequently with the Secretary General and with other USUN personnel who were in almost daily contact with Undersecretary General Ralph Bunche and other UN officials concerned with the operation. The military officers at USUN performed a liaison function with the defense Department in Washington in processing UN requests for logistical support and supplies, working closely with political officers at USUN and the State Department.

Thus, the United States was influential with both Hammarskjöld and Thant in carrying out the operation; however, its influence with them arose not so much from its logistical and financial support as from the fact that the American interest in stability in the Congo and a constitutional solution to the internal conflict there corresponded to a remarkable degree with the central objective of the UN effort. Good personal relationships between USUN and Secretariat personnel, particularly Stevenson with Thant, made the cooperation smoother and more effective, but the decisive factor was the compatibility of interest.[30]

The UN Operation in the Congo ended in June 1964; however, the UN's civilian operation continued. Begun in 1960, this operation aimed to keep intact transport and communications; to sustain a decent level of public health; to further education and public administration; and to develop industry and agriculture. It was financed largely from the UN Congo Fund, made up of voluntary contributions from 20 governments. The United

States at first contributed about three-fourths and later about half of the total; the Soviet Union made no contribution.

Much more serious was the refusal of the Soviet Union, its satellites, and France to pay their share of the expenses of the UN Force in the Congo (discussed later in this chapter).

THE BAY OF PIGS

"The integrity and credibility of Adlai Stevenson," President Kennedy told Arthur Schlesinger in April 1961, "constitute one of our great national assets. I don't want anything to be done which might jeopardize that."[31] Like the rest of the Bay of Pigs fiasco, this Kennedy aim went awry.

In New York, Adlai Stevenson was getting ready for a General Assembly debate of a Cuban charge that the United States had aggressive intentions against Cuba. Schlesinger briefed Stevenson on the invasion plans but left him with the impression that no action would take place during the UN discussion of the Cuban item. Stevenson wholly disapproved of the plan, regretted that he had been given no opportunity to comment on it, and believed that it would cause infinite trouble. But, if it was national policy, he was prepared to make out the best possible case.

After the Saturday (April 15) air strike, Raul Roa, the Cuban foreign minister, succeeded in advancing the Cuban item, scheduled for the following Monday, to an emergency session of the UN Political Committee that afternoon. In Washington, Harlan Cleveland tried to ascertain the facts about the strike. His office called the Bureau of Inter-American affairs, which in turn called the CIA. Word promptly and definitely came back that it was the work of genuine defectors, and Cleveland passed this information on to Stevenson. A few moments later Stevenson told the UN: "these two planes, to the best of our knowledge, were Castro's own air force planes and, according to the pilots, they took off from Castro's own air force fields."

Unfortunately, the CIA had not been truthful with the concerned bureaus of the State Department. Rusk, remorseful at the position into which State had thrust its UN ambassador, now resolved that the Cuban adventure should not be permitted further to jeopardize the larger interests of U.S. foreign policy.

The collapse of the cover story brought the question of the second air strike into new focus. The President and the secretary understood this strike as the one that would take place simultaneously with the landings and have the appearance of coming from the airstrip on the beach. It had slid by in the briefings, everyone assuming that it would be masked by the cover story. But there could be no easy attribution to defectors now. Nor did the fact that planes were B-26s flown by Cuban pilots save the situation; despite the great to-do about "Cubanizing" the operation, they would still be U.S. planes in the eyes of the UN. Rusk, after his talks with Stevenson, concluded that a second Nicaraguan strike would put the United States in an untenable position internationally and that no further strikes should be launched until the planes could fly (or appear to fly) from the beachhead. Bundy agreed, and they called the President, who directed that the second air strike be canceled.[32]

The Bay of Pigs invasion was, of course, a disaster. Kennedy's decision against further air strikes was not based solely on a desire to avoid additional embarrassment for Stevenson at the UN; it was determined in the light of worldwide American interests and the intangible but important value of world opinion. It had also become clear that, with or without air cover, the invasion was doomed to failure. Yet the role of the UN as a mirror of world reaction and Stevenson's acute discomfiture were factors in Kennedy's decision to avoid further action that would compound the error.

Surprisingly the standing of both Stevenson and the United States at the UN recovered quickly. It was generally perceived that Stevenson had not deliberately lied but had himself been duped, and there was much sympathy for him. As for the American standing, the United States was perceived to have stumbled but not to have embarked on a generally malign course in the world. It was not yet seriously involved in Vietnam and had a record of support for most majority objectives in the UN, such as economic development and the UN operation in the Congo. Even on colonial issues the United States was considered to be a potential moderating influence on the European colonial powers. At the fall 1961 session of the UN General Assembly, Kennedy's address was received with great enthusiasm and Stevenson's prestige was high.[33] Indeed, in my fifteen sessions at the UN General Assembly, 1956–1970, I cannot recall any other time that U.S. prestige was riding as high as in 1961—nor, as an observer, have I witnessed any since 1970.

THE CUBAN MISSILE CRISIS

The next crisis found Stevenson both fully informed and functioning as a key member of the Kennedy team, in sharp contrast with his role in the Bay of Pigs fiasco.

By September 1962, the United States was aware that Soviet aid to Cuba included surface-to-air missiles, but Washington thought they were essentially defensive and not threatening to American security. By October 15, however, air and sea surveillance revealed evidence of a secret buildup of sites for offensive nuclear missiles capable of reaching targets in the United States and most of the Western Hemisphere.

Since the missiles had not been fully emplaced, time was of the essence, and the exploration of alternative responses went on feverishly. The President worked with an ad hoc Executive Committee that included Stevenson.[34] The main alternatives that emerged were an air strike against the missile sites or a "quarantine" against Soviet shipments of military and related supplies. Attorney General Robert Kennedy, the President's brother, passionately opposed an air strike as a "Pearl Harbor in reverse."[35] Stevenson also opposed an air strike and agreed on the quarantine. By October 19, the President and the Executive Committee decided on it.

During the Executive Committee's discussion of alternatives, Stevenson emphasized the importance of diplomatic measures along with the quarantine. In this vein he suggested the possibility of a demilitarized, neutralized Cuba whose territorial integrity we would join in guaranteeing through the UN. This would have meant giving up the U.S. base at Guantanamo, but it would also have meant removal of the Soviet military presence from Cuba. He also suggested that the United States might agree to give up its Jupiter missile bases in Italy and Turkey. In 1961 the Secretary of Defense had urged removal of these bases on the grounds that they were obsolescent and vulnerable.[36]

The President, however, regarded any such political program as premature; he wanted to concentrate on a single issue—the removal of the Soviet missiles. Nevertheless, some of Stevenson's tactical advice was followed. For example, the President postponed his address announcing the quarantine to the nation from Sunday, October 21, to Monday evening in order to inform the members of the Organization of American States (OAS) of the action before it was under way. Kennedy also agreed to Stevenson's suggestion that the United States call for an emergency meeting of the UN Security Council.

When the Security Council met on October 23, Stevenson was able to announce that the OAS had just adopted, with nineteen affirmative votes, a resolution calling for the immediate dismantling and withdrawal from Cuba of all missiles and other weapons with any offensive capability and recommending that member states take measures individually and collectively, including the use of armed forces that they might deem necessary, to insure that the government of Cuba could not continue to receive from the "Sino-Soviet power" military material and related supplies that could threaten the peace and security of a continent.[37] This endorsement of the U.S. quarantine was, of course, a substantial plus for the American political position.

Stevenson's suggestions for a possible trade-off of bases led some members of the Executive Committee to consider him too "soft." Accordingly, John McCloy, a Republican veteran of arms control negotiations, was added to the delegation, and he assisted Stevenson in the negotiations with the Soviets and U Thant into the spring of 1963.

As far as the presentation of the U.S. case was concerned, the hard-liners had no cause for concern. Stevenson was at his eloquent best in explaining the U.S. actions and in his indictment of Soviet aggression and duplicity.[38]

At the October 23 session, draft resolutions—by the United States on the one hand and by the Soviet Union and Cuba on the other—each condemned, and demanded the revocation of, the actions of the opposite party. Both drafts also, and significantly, urged the Council to call on the parties to enter into negotiations to "remove the existing threat" to peace or to "reestablish a normal situation." They were, in short, seeking a means of escape from an apparently closed situation. The Security Council members provided one by hearing the parties and then adjourning without voting on any resolution. This allowed the start of direct negotiations by the Soviet and American delegates under the Council's aegis and in consultation with U Thant.

On October 24 the Secretary General appealed to both Kennedy and Khrushchev to refrain from aggravating the situation. To facilitate negotiations, he proposed the voluntary suspension of Soviet shipments, of American quarantine measures, and of Cuban construction of installations. The President declared, however, that only removal of the weapons causing the crisis could bring about a peaceful solution.

The Secretary General then proposed, on October 25, that, to permit discussions, Soviet ships should stay away from the announced interception areas for the next few days and that U.S. vessels should avoid direct confrontation with Soviet ships. On October 26 the Soviet premier told U Thant that he had so ordered the Soviet ships; and the President, that American vessels would do everything possible to avoid confrontation if the ships stayed away. Work on the missile sites continued to aggravate the situation. Between October 26 and October 28, a number of messages crisscrossed between President and Premier. The end result was an undertaking by Khrushchev to dismantle the offending weapons and return them to the Soviet Union, subject to UN verification; and by Kennedy that, if these commitments were implemented and no further weapons introduced (subject to verification), he would lift the quarantine and give assurances against any invasion.

It is important to put the role of the UN and Stevenson in perspective. The crucial factors in resolving the crisis were the American military superiority at that time, particularly in nuclear missiles and in the Caribbean area (by contrast, a U.S. military action against Soviet intervention in Hungary in 1956 would have been infinitely more complex and risky); the choice of a tactic, quarantine, that allowed time for the Kremlin to reflect on the situation and retreat with some face-saving; and Khrushchev's willingness to back down rather than risk a nuclear holocaust.

The crucial negotiations were bilateral between Washington and Moscow, yet the UN made a significant ancillary contribution to U.S. policy objectives. Stevenson observed in a statement to the Senate Committee on

Foreign Relations that the UN had been useful in the following ways: (1) it provided a world forum; (2) the Secretary General's intervention on October 25 led to the diversion of Soviet ships that had been headed for Cuba and interception by the U.S. Navy—"an indispensable first step in the peaceful resolution of the Cuban crisis"; (3) the UN was the site of negotiations between the Soviets and Stevenson and McCloy; (4) the Secretary General's offer to assure removal of the missiles by UN inspection was accepted by the Soviet Union and the United States; unfortunately, it was rejected by Castro, and the United States had to use its own means of verification.[39]

Ruth Russell points out that "the obvious role of the United Nations as a forum was useful in rallying the moral support of other governments in favor of peaceful settlement; and that its somewhat less obvious role, operating especially through the secretary-general, was even more useful in allowing the nuclear dialogue to be reopened without either side appearing to concede its case."[40]

With the world poised on the brink of nuclear war, even these ancillary contributions must be considered of substantial value. As for Stevenson himself, the decision on what action to take in all likelihood would have been the same whether or not he had been involved in the Executive Committee. Where he did make an important contribution was in improving the American public posture, both by advising Kennedy on timing and procedures after the quarantine decision had been made and by his brilliant performance in the Security Council.

Ironically, Stevenson, who had performed admirably, was to suffer severe embarrassment about his alleged "softness." The incident is described as follows by a Stevenson biographer, Bert Cochran:

In early December 1962 the *Saturday Evening Post* published an article by Stewart Alsop and Charles Bartlett purporting to disclose what went on inside the government during the crisis. The two authors, who obviously had received inside information, made the sensational charge that Stevenson was the lone dissenter from the crucial decision reached. They quoted an unnamed official as saying, "Adlai wanted another Munich. He wanted to trade Turkish, Italian and British missile bases for the Cuban bases." It also stated that "tough-minded" John McCloy had been assigned to work with Stevenson in the negotiations with the Russians at the UN because Stevenson was too weak to be entrusted with the responsibility. The article naturally made headlines and was the talk of the corridors for weeks thereafter. It was generally assumed that the White House had collaborated in supplying the information, and that the President was trying to force Stevenson's resignation. Newspapermen recalled that a previous Bartlett story had presaged the removal of Chester Bowles from the State Department. This interpretation was given further credence when Pierre Salinger, the White House press secretary, in response to inquiries, put out a statement that loftily acknowledged that Stevenson had "strongly supported the decision taken by the President," but left unanswered the accusation that Stevenson had opposed the otherwise unanimous decision and had advocated another Munich. Stevenson dealt with the article in a television interview. *He said it was "wrong in literally every detail" and that he had supported the idea of a blockade days before the decision was made* [italics mine]. "What the article doesn't say is that I opposed an invasion of Cuba at the risk of nuclear war until the peace-keeping machinery of the United Nations had been used." He was disturbed by the President's failure to back him up. He told Schlesinger, who was serving as the mediator between them, that Kennedy need not have been so "circuitous" if he wanted him to resign. When Schlesinger related this, Kennedy hotly denied that he had any such wish and said he would regard Stevenson's resignation "as a disaster." He explained that "from a realistic political viewpoint, it is better for me to have Adlai in the government than out." It is possible that the press attack was meant to cut Stevenson down to size rather than to force him out.

By this time it had become clear that the intrigue to ruin him was backfiring, and was more damaging to the President's image than to the Ambassador's prestige. Kennedy had to make repeated statements expressing his confidence in Stevenson, culminating in the release of a laudatory personal letter. "The reaction was so intense and so strongly in Mr. Stevenson's favor," commented the *New York Times*, "that the President had to keep him on, even if he had wanted otherwise."[41]

Even so, the incident hardly indicates any real closeness between Kennedy and Stevenson.

As Cochran notes, Stevenson was not against the cold war or standing up to the Soviets when the situation demanded it. His differences with hard-liners in Washington were largely over tactics.[42] He did advocate greater flexibility in our relations with Moscow and Peking, raising questions over how long we should try to bar the latter from a seat at the UN. Kennedy shared Stevenson's desire for flexibility. In his first year in office Kennedy thought it would be useful for Australia and the United Kingdom to float a two-China resolution in the UN General Assembly, but domestic American politics made it difficult for the United States to move. Instead, a tactical device was adopted, obtaining a General Assembly decision that any substantive decision to change the representation of China was an important question requiring a two-thirds majority. This tactical maneuver, designed to gain a year until circumstances became more propitious, actually protected Taiwan's sole occupancy of the China seat for a decade.

STEVENSON, LYNDON JOHNSON, AND VIETNAM

After Kennedy's death, President Lyndon Johnson was effusive in welcoming Stevenson into the new administration. He said he knew that the late President had not been consulting him but said that was going to be changed. He also told Stevenson he wanted him to play a large role in the formation of policy.[43]

At first, relations were better. Johnson was of the same generation and,

Stevenson thought, understood him better. Stevenson applauded Johnson's choice of Humphrey as a running mate. But Johnson in fact turned out to be less interested in the UN than Kennedy had been. Stevenson soon found that he was having considerably less effective influence on policy than he had before, for all of Johnson's repeated expressions of admiration and need of him. Schlesinger observed: "It turned out that he was in worse shape with Johnson than he had been with Kennedy because Rusk quickly got more power," a judgment concurred in by Harlan Cleveland and supported by my own impressions at USUN. As Johnson became increasingly preoccupied with Vietnam, he relied more and more on Rusk, McNamara, and Bundy, his inner circle.[44] U Thant described Johnson's judgment of Stevenson as follows: "He had no sense of correct judgment of public opinion; his evaluation of events, both domestic and foreign, usually turned out to be incorrect. In the President's opinion, Mr. Stevenson was just an idealist with his head in the clouds." Stevenson himself noted that, though Johnson continued to urge him to stay on, he had little opportunity for close personal relationships or "low down" quiet talks with the President.[45]

The two men were quite different in background and style. Johnson considered Stevenson an effete aristocrat, and Stevenson thought Johnson's style was "cornpone." Also, Stevenson was disturbed over the American intervention in the Dominican Republic in 1965. But the most serious problem for their relationship was Vietnam.

Stevenson did not oppose U.S. intervention in Vietnam. He considered it part of the overall policy to contain communist expansion, which, in common with most postwar liberal Democrats, he supported. In the Security Council meetings of August 1964 he called the Tonkin Gulf incident "a planned, deliberate aggression against vessels in international waters" and assured the Council that the United States wanted "no wider war." The Council meetings were inconclusive, in part because Hanoi refused to participate despite the fact that the United States had raised no objection when the Soviets proposed that they be invited.

Stevenson agreed with Johnson and his Rusk-McNamara-Bundy triumvirate that Hanoi should be prevented from taking over South Vietnam by force. His chief and often agonizing difference with them was over the desirability and feasibility of a negotiated settlement. After the Tonkin Gulf incident Stevenson agreed that the United States should first increase its military efforts in South Vietnam to "give clear evidence of our firm purpose," then go to the UN Security Council and ask for a UN observer group to report on "infiltrations" and ways of enforcing the 1954 Geneva accords. Johnson had little faith in getting much from the Security Council, given the fact that the Soviets and the French were opposed to its taking action on Vietnam. The UN secretary general apparently felt the same way; on February 12, 1965, Stevenson reported that Thant urged reconvening the Geneva Conference parties to the 1954 agreement.[46] Replies from

Washington made it clear that the United States was not then ready to go to such a conference.

Stevenson felt even more frustrated that, in his view, Washington had deliberately neglected chances for direct negotiations sought by the Secretary General. U Thant first suggested to Secretary Rusk secret meetings between U.S. and Hanoi representatives, then sounded out Hanoi via the Soviets. According to Thant, Hanoi agreed within three weeks. Stevenson, after consulting Washington, told Thant nothing could be done until after the U.S. elections. Five months passed with no response from Washington. Then Stevenson, on his own initiative on January 18, 1965, saw Thant again. Stevenson then informed Washington that, according to Thant, all arrangements were completed for an ambassadorial-level meeting in Rangoon, pending U.S. concurrence and the naming of an emissary. On January 28 Washington declined on the grounds that holding such bilateral talks would cause the fall of the Saigon government and that the United States doubted Hanoi really wanted the talks. This angered Thant and bothered Stevenson.[47]

Washington's objections cannot be dismissed lightly. It is a tricky business to negotiate with the enemy of one's ally without the presence of the ally. And although U Thant was an honest man of goodwill (I knew him for ten years and some of his close associates even longer), it is far from certain that he had a clear commitment from Hanoi. Rusk was skeptical because Thant apparently did not know that Washington was providing secret large-scale aid to the government of Burma in its fight against communist rebels and could get corroborative information from that government about any proposed meetings in its capital if they were for real.[48] Moreover, Washington had seen the latest report of Blair Seborn, Canadian member of the International Control Commission in Vietnam, indicating that Hanoi was not prepared for serious talks to end its involvement in South Vietnam. Indeed Hanoi later denied that it had suggested any negotiations to Thant.[49] And on April 4, 1965, Thant told the United States he had received a message from Peking through the Algerians that the UN should not become involved in Southeast Asia and that Peking had no interest in a visit by Thant. Hanoi had also sent word that Thant would not be welcome there.[50]

In any case, in January 1965 Thant had disclosed that the source of his report that Hanoi would be prepared to carry out bilateral negotiations in Rangoon was a Russian agent. At the time neither the Soviet ambassador to the United States nor the Soviet representative to the UN knew about the maneuver, another factor in undermining the credibility of the report. Martin observes: "In addition Rusk—and probably Johnson as well—seems to have taken the general view that Thant was soft, wobbly and imprecise and to have lacked wholehearted confidence in him as an intermediary." Martin also provides a brief compendium of insiders' interpretations that indicate why Thant's initiative gained so little credence with the President and his top advisers. Moreover, there were many other efforts to arrange negotiations at the time, and Johnson did not like "negotiations from weakness."[51]

Unfortunately, Thant made numerous public statements about Vietnam that annoyed Washington, especially Rusk; as a result, Washington had little confidence in him. Thant might have been more successful in his efforts if he had emulated the public discretion combined with private negotiations that Hammarskjöld had used, for example, in securing the release of the American fliers from Peking. Undoubtedly the public utterance that jarred Johnson and Rusk the most was Thant's February 12, 1965 statement that the American people were not being given the "true facts" about Vietnam. It is now clear that Thant was right, but the statement was not the kind a secretary general should make in public when he wants the cooperation of the government concerned. Rusk's irritation with U Thant's public statements was long lasting. I recall being in Arthur Goldberg's office some years later, when Rusk called up and asked: "Have you heard what your client said today?"

Along with his frustration over the failure of Thant's efforts to bring about negotiations, Stevenson was deeply disturbed about America's continued large-scale bombing of North Vietnam. Johnson ordered the sustained bombing in mid-February 1965, and it continued, with a week's pause in December 1965 and January 1966, throughout Johnson's term. (There had also been a strike against Hanoi in early February 1965, while Soviet Premier Kosygin was there, in retaliation for a Viet Cong attack on U.S. barracks in Pleiku—an action not likely to encourage Soviet help in bringing about a negotiated settlement.) Stevenson believed, as did Thant, that the bombings would harden Hanoi's resistance to negotiations.

Although Stevenson was deeply disturbed by the bombings and ardently sought negotiations for peace, there is no evidence that he disagreed with the basic American policy of preventing Hanoi from taking over South Vietnam by force. On June 21, 1965, a few weeks before his death, Stevenson met at USUN with a group of intellectuals who urged him to resign in protest against the U.S. policy in Vietnam. On this issue, as on many others, he saw both sides of the question, agonized over the consequences of each, and was profoundly disturbed when individuals whom he respected disagreed with him on an important issue, but he did not accept his critics' viewpoint. In a letter to one of the group, Paul Goodman, drafted in Libertyville over the July 4 weekend but never mailed, he wrote: "Whatever criticisms can be made over the details and emphasis of American foreign policy, its purpose and direction are sound." He went on to urge that there should be no attempt to change the tacitly agreed East-West frontiers by force (containment) and that one should move from this position of precarious stability toward agreed international procedures for settling differences, building an international juridical and policing system, and working toward a genuine economic and social community. He stressed the need to check "Chinese expansionism." He believed in a negotiated peace based on the internationalization of the whole area's security and argued that a retreat in Asia or anywhere else would not help to move toward this ideal.[52]

Stevenson expressed the same viewpoint on BBC television on July 10, 1965 two days before his death. With respect to Vietnam, he said: "As we did in Europe, we shall have to draw a line between the Communist and non-Communist world areas so that neither power system can force a change by force."[53] Shortly before that he had written his son, Adlai III, about the many people who had urged him to resign in protest against the administration's Vietnam policy; he resented their assumption that he disagreed with the policy. Further, even if he did disagree, it was by no means certain that the most effective act was resignation; it might be better to stay and try to influence policy.

While accepting the doctrine that North Vietnam must be prevented from taking over South Vietnam by force, even at the cost of U.S. military intervention, Stevenson differed with the President on the policy of military escalation. He argued that escalation carried more risk of worsening the situation than of persuading Hanoi to compromise. He thought that talks would be less risky than military escalation, even though Hanoi had given no indication that it would settle for anything less than control over all Vietnam. He was proved right about the risks of military escalation; however, by June 11, 1965, he had concluded that "Peking and Hanoi are not interested in a peaceful solution as long as there is a prospect of winning by a military decision."[54]

With hindsight it is clear that the fundamental error was the tragic misperception by American policy makers of the true relationship between the Chinese and Vietnamese. A unified, Communist Vietnam has not become an instrument of Chinese aggression that would topple dominoes in Thailand, Malaysia, Singapore, Indonesia, and the Philippines, as the United States feared in the '60s. On the contrary, China and Vietnam now pursue mutually hostile policies and even fought an undeclared war in 1979. It is evident that a Communist regime in all of Vietnam, or even all of Indochina, while bringing massive suffering and gross human rights violations to the people there, does not constitute a threat to American security—the only kind of threat that could have justified such a massive intervention.

Another tragic irony is the fact that Lyndon Johnson, who had opposed American military involvement in Vietnam when he was Senate Majority Leader, was the President who ordered the bombing and increased American troop strength in Vietnam from 16,000 to over 500,000. Johnson became convinced that, whether it was right or wrong to plant the American flag in Vietnam, the United States could not afford to lose face and credibility by leaving as a loser. As a result he took steps that cost tens of thousands of lives and spent over $150 billion that could have financed his War on Poverty and that fueled disastrous inflation. The costs of the American economy and social structure were enormous. The losses in international standing and moral position in the world are difficult to calculate but certainly substantial.

THE DOMINICAN CRISIS

Stevenson was disturbed by the U.S.-OAS intervention in the Dominican Republic in the spring of 1965, shortly before his death. He did not object to sending in a small detachment of marines to protect American citizens caught in the swirl of a civil war, but he was dismayed as the size of the force grew to 20,000 and President Johnson announced that the troops were there to prevent "another Cuba." Still, Stevenson himself, on instructions from Washington, stated in the Security Council: "The American nations will not permit the establishment of another Communist government in the Western Hemisphere,"[55] the essence of what has come to be known as the Johnson doctrine.

According to Eric Severeid, reporting on a conversation with Stevenson shortly before his death, Stevenson's objection may have been tactical. He reportedly asked Severeid: "Couldn't the President have waited, say three days, so we could round up more Latin American support?" Stevenson also questioned the size of the force but apparently accepted Severeid's explanation of the need for it in view of the size of the barrier to be policed between the two fighting forces.[56]

Stevenson was also concerned about the precedent set for other regional organizations when the intervention became an OAS operation, a concern prompted by the UN Secretary General's attitude. U Thant said: "If a particular regional organization under the terms of its own constitution, deems it fit to take certain enforcement action in its own region, it naturally follows that other regional organizations should be considered competent, because of the precedent, to take certain enforcement action within their own regions."[57] Thant specifically mentioned the Organization of African Unity and the League of Arab States; however, the next action came from another regional group, the Warsaw Pact, in 1968. An interesting parallel has been drawn between the Johnson doctrine, justifying the 1965 OAS action in the Dominican Republic, and the Brezhnev doctrine, which explained the August 1968 invasion of Czechoslovakia by the Soviet Union on the grounds that fellow socialist states had a right to protect another socialist state against counterrevolution.[58]

In the Dominican case, the Soviet Union promptly brought the issue to the UN Security Council, condemning Washington's "armed intervention" as a violation of the Charter. It demanded immediate withdrawal of United States forces and denounced the Inter-American Force as illegal.

The crucial question was whether the action constituted enforcement action that, according to Article 53, would require prior authorization by the Security Council. Stevenson argued that the Inter-American Force was not aimed "at asserting any authority to govern any part of the Dominican Republic but were intended to preserve for the people . . . their right to choose their own government free of outside interference."[59] Thus, he contended, the OAS fell under Article 52, as appropriate regional action for the maintenance of international peace and security, and did not require prior Council approval.

The United States at first argued against any UN action, on the ground that it would complicate OAS activities. Uruguay, which had voted against the force in the OAS—where the United States had barely mustered the necessary two-thirds majority—worked in the Security Council for a compromise that would insert the Council into the situation without condemning the OAS action. Lacking strong Latin American support, the United States accepted a resolution that called for a strict cease-fire and invited the secretary general to report to the Council on the situation.[60]

Thant sent a small group to Santo Domingo, headed by Antonio Mayobre of Venezuela and including the secretary general's military adviser. This group was too small and its mandate too weak to interfere with the OAS activity; nevertheless, there was initially considerable mutual suspicion. Finally, a year after the initial intervention, during which there was considerable rightist opposition to the program of the Dominican Provisional Government, the promised national elections were held June 1, 1965, and a moderate constitutional government was elected, headed by Joaquin Balaguer. All three presidential candidates had called for the withdrawal of the Inter-American Force and the last troops left by September.

During the year there were sporadic, repeated meetings of the Security Council convened on the initiative of the Soviets every time the leader of the Dominican leftists asked for one. The meetings led nowhere, and there was little interest in them, either of the public or the UN delegations. Finally, in October 1966 the Dominican government expressed its appreciation for UN interest but declared that the Security Council's objectives had been accomplished and that, therefore, the UN mission be withdrawn—which it was forthwith.[61]

An interesting viewpoint was expressed by Walt Rostow. He writes that Antonio Mayobre (the UN representative in Santo Domingo) "had reacted initially with some passion against the intervention . . . but by the early months of 1966 he had come to the view that the process of democratization in the Dominican Republic had been set forward by fifteen years and with rare grace, he was prepared to tell this to me and others."[62]

Stevenson, however, had lingering doubts about the U.S.-OAS action right up to the time of his death. John B. Martin, one of his biographers, could find no comments on it in either his files or his public correspondence. (As noted, Stevenson was an effective advocate of U.S. policy in the UN Security Council.) Martin, who was ambassador to the Dominican Republic, 1962–64, and who served as President Johnson's personal representative to help in bringing peace in 1965, writes that Stevenson was perplexed but "not upset." Martin explained the U.S. operation, and "Stevenson seemed to accept the explanation."[63] Yet at a dinner in Paris shortly before his death, at which CBS correspondent David Schoenbrun was present, Stevenson called the operation "a massive blunder"—which Schoenbrun reported. Averell Harriman and Francis Plimpton thought Schoenbrun had misunderstood Stevenson, whom they had both known well for decades. Probably Stevenson had used hyperbole, not expecting to be quoted; even so, his remarks showed lingering, agonizing doubt.[64] The Secretary General of the UN, U Thant, not only shared Stevenson's doubt; he considered the U.S. intervention a blunder that furnished a pretext for Soviet intervention in Czechoslovakia in 1968.[65]

THE FINANCIAL CRISIS AND ARTICLE 19

The UN Operation of the Congo (ONUC) was kept going, as noted earlier, primarily by a confluence of African desires to get the Belgians out and the American desire to keep the Soviets out of the Congo. Thus, despite Soviet opposition after the fall of Patrice Lumumba in September 1960, the operation continued. But the Soviets, their satellites, and France manifested their opposition by refusing to pay their budget assessments for ONUC.

Since the Soviets had also refused to pay their assessments for the UN Emergency Force in the Middle East, the financial situation of the UN became critical. By the end of 1961 the UN had unpaid obligations of about $110 million and unpaid assessments of about $80 million. These figures might appear small when compared with the U.S. federal budget and national debt; however, in UN terms the deficit was huge and threatened to end ONUC. The UN's annual budget in 1961 was $73 million, and ONUC was costing about $110 million per year. Unlike national governments, the UN cannot print money to cover deficits. National contingents provided for ONUC were going unpaid, as were bills for material and other operating costs.

To keep ONUC going, USUN came up with a new idea for the UN—a bond issue. Phil Klutznick describes its origin as follows:

The idea of a Bond Issue was knocked around in our shop at the Mission with Al Bender [senior adviser on financial affairs] and his people having considerable to do with the origination of the idea. It took on a rather limited form at the beginning. I discussed it with Adlai who suggested I pursue it. As you know, Adlai *had little patience or time for the fiscal affairs of the UN* [italics mine]. The whole idea was given more character when we nearly folded the Congo Operation in the Spring, 1961. You will recall that all-night session where early in the morning we finally got a vote to finance the operation.[66] It became clear at that time that it was probably the last vote we could get if we did not come up with a better financing medium.

I spent some time with the Bureau of the Budget and with Harlan Cleveland and between us we finally got the green light from the Bureau. The question then arose whose initiative was it to be. I argued for the Secretary General to accept the idea and make it his own. Adlai and I had a date with the Secretary General [U Thant] for one late morning. He was coming in from Washington. At the last minute, he had to delay his arrival. He called me and asked me to go see the Secretary myself, which I did. The Secretary General was very sympathetic in the idea but wanted us to father it. I called his attention to the fact that it would be a difficult one at best and he was in a honeymoon period, which made it a certainty it could pass if he fathered it. He called in Eugene Black [President of the World Bank] for a session in which we went over the whole matter and finally he reached the conclusion that he would propose it to the Fifth Committee, which he did. That was the beginning.[67] (U Thant "fathered" the bond idea so thoroughly he claimed credit for it in his memoirs, not even mentioning the U.S. role.) Thant, like Stevenson, had little interest in, or understanding of, UN finances, as his account of the Article 19 situation reveals.[68]

That was the beginning. First there was a long struggle in the General Assembly, which, on December 20, 1961, finally authorized the secretary general to issue United Nations bonds up to a limit of $200 million and "to utilize the proceeds from the sale of such bonds for the purposes normally related to the Working Capital Fund," that is, for paying ONUC expenses, inter alia. The bonds were to be repayable in 25 annual installments, bearing interest at 2 percent per annum on the principal amount outstanding; with the interest and amortization charges to be included in the UN's regular budget beginning in 1963.[69] The United States pledged to match any purchases by all other countries combined and actually bought $85 million out of a total of $170 million.

The next step was to gain approval from a wary U.S. Congress. Just before the Senate hearings, Klutznick was asked to go to other countries to sell the bond issue and Francis Plimpton took over. He writes: "I have always suspected that the reason was that Senator Aiken had spread the word that I was the real father of the bond issue."[70] Congress finally approved but insisted on a commitment that delinquent members would have to pay their assessments or lose their right to vote under Article 19 of the UN Charter if their arrears exceeded more than two years' assessments.[71]

Thus, the bond issue assured continuation of ONUC and laid the groundwork for the Article 19 controversy that threatened to paralyze the UN in 1964 and 1965.

Those who supported the authority of the General Assembly were encouraged when the International Court of Justice, following a request from the Assembly for an advisory opinion, stated in a majority opinion of July 20, 1962 that the expenditures authorized by the Assembly for peacekeeping operations in the Congo and the Middle East "constitute expenses of the organization within the meaning of Article 17, paragraph 2, of the United Nations Charter."[72] Five months later, on December 19, 1962, the General Assembly accepted the opinion of the International Court of Justice (ICJ) by a vote of 76 to 17 (including France and eleven communist states), with 8 abstentions.[73]

By the time the nineteenth General Assembly would open in the fall of 1964, the Soviet Union and a number of other states would have arrears amounting to more than two years' assessment. By January 1, 1965, France would be in the same situation. Article 19 of the United Nations Charter provides:

A Member of the United Nations which is in arrears in the payment of its financial contributions of the Organization shall have no vote in the General Assembly if the amount of its arrears equals or exceed the amount of the contributions due from it for the preceding two full years. The General Assembly may, nevertheless, permit such a Member to vote if it is satisfied that the failure to pay is due to conditions beyond the control of the Member.

So the battle was joined. The Soviets and the French, despite the International Court of Justice opinion and its acceptance by an overwhelming majority, were adamant on their refusal to pay. The real conflict was with the authority of the General Assembly under the Charter, which it was in the interest of the Third World majority to uphold. Yet, because of the commitment to the U.S. Congress when the bond issue was approved, the energy of USUN, and the tendency of the media to play up Soviet-American confrontations, the controversy appeared to be a cold-war issue.

Having been involved with the issue from July 1964 to the denouement, I know that USUN did not perceive the action as an anti-Soviet maneuver, nor was that the attitude of those we dealt with in the State Department. Unless the arrears were paid, there was no way to reimburse the states that had provided contingents for ONUC and UNEF. These included poorer countries, such as Ethiopia, India, Tunisia, Indonesia, and Morocco, as well as Canada and the Nordic countries. How could one have future peacekeeping operations on a sound basis if the authority of the General Assembly to levy assessments was successfully challenged? If the General Assembly itself failed to enforce its authority under Article 19 in this instance, how could it do so in the future? And there was also the commitment to Congress.

The Soviets and the French did not ask for exception under the second sentence of Article 19, that is, if the Assembly "is satisfied that the failure to pay is due to conditions beyond the control of the Member." They argued, despite the ICJ opinion and its acceptance by the General Assembly, that the assessments for ONUC and UNEF were not mandatory because the operations were, in their view, not conducted in accordance with Chapter VII of the UN Charter; hence, they had no obligation to pay. In their view only the Security Council could take action for the maintenance of peace and security, including financing.[74] (Curiously, France paid its assessments for UNEF, which had been authorized by the General Assembly, but not for ONUC, authorized by the Security Council. The Soviets paid for neither.)

As far back as March 6, 1964, Stevenson proposed to the Soviets that they pay enough to satisfy Article 19 on the assurance that they would not have to pay for future peacekeeping operations of which they did not approve. This offer was certainly not made in a cold-war spirit. On March 21 the Soviets rejected it. Congress then passed a joint resolution calling upon Stevenson to insure that the defaulting countries paid up or Article 19 applied.[75]

At USUN during the summer and early fall of 1964 we spent hundreds of hours trying to devise formulas under which the Soviets and French could contribute amounts sufficient to obviate the application of Article 19, while still maintaining their positions of principle. We even devised schemes for American contributions that would not require new congressional appropriations, such as cancellation of a UN debt for certain U.S. services provided for ONUC and of "surplus accounts," representing assessments paid during a period when ONUC expenses were met from the proceeds of the bond issue. In fact, the United States has never collected a dime on these accounts anyway, because the deficit remained. Yet the amount nominally involved would have matched the sum in new funds that the Soviets would have to pay to avoid the applicability of Article 19. Nevertheless the Soviets, when approached by an intermediary group consisting of the Afghan, Nigerian, Norwegian, and Venezuelan ambassadors, would not promise any specific sum. Instead, they skillfully dropped hints of willingness to make a voluntary contribution, thus weakening the resolve of the smaller countries, but never mentioned how much, when, or how.

It became clear that most Third World countries, while agreeing with the Western position (minus France, Spain, and Portugal) on principle, were genuinely worried about the prospect that the Soviets, if deprived of their vote in the General Assembly, would leave the UN. For example, Ambassador El Kony of Egypt told Plimpton in my presence that Egypt needed the Soviet veto in the Security Council and would, therefore, oppose any action that would jeopardize the Soviet presence in the UN. Yet Egypt very much wanted UNEF to continue and had a stake, as a Third World country, in maintaining the authority of the General Assembly. At USUN we were convinced that the Soviets would find a way to pay if the Third World countries stood firm. Clearly, many African and Asian states did not see it that way, fearing a Soviet walkout, and their unwillingness to go to a showdown proved decisive.

Because of the widespread reluctance toward a showdown, U Thant suggested, after polling the membership, that the opening of the nineteenth session of the General Assembly be postponed from November 10 to December 1. There was general concurrence and no opposition from Washington. On November 13 Adlai Stevenson stated publicly that "voluntary payments could be made without prejudice to the Soviets or anyone else's legal views. Any arrangements for such payments consistent with the Charter and satisfactory to the Secretary General will be satisfactory to the United States."[76]

A crucial factor was the legal position of the man destined to preside at the opening of the nineteenth session, Ambassador Carlos Sosa Rodriquez of Venezuela, with whom Francis Plimpton and other USUN people had a number of meetings. Sosa, while believing that Article 19 should be applied against the delinquents, held that the General Assembly must make the decision. As an important question, this would require a two-thirds majority. Our head count indicated that we were close to that figure, but there was a real question whether we could get to a showdown vote at all. The U.S. view was that the loss of vote provision became automatic, since Article 19 states that a member "shall have no vote if the amount of its arrears exceeds the amount of its contributions due from it for the preceding two years." As a precedent, Mohammed Zafrula Khan, president of the fourth special session of the General Assembly in 1963, had ruled that Haiti's loss of vote was automatic unless and until it paid enough to remove the applicability of Article 19.[77] Should the President's ruling be challenged, the challengers would need a majority to set his ruling aside. Thus, only half the votes would be required to uphold Article 19's application instead of the two-thirds required if the General Assembly had to take implementing action. Sosa, however, held firmly to his legal position.

Another factor that might have made a difference was the airdrop of Belgian paratroopers from American planes on Stanleyville on November 14, 1964, to rescue a group of white hostages from a leftist rebel group. Since the operation, whether intentionally or not, also helped Moise Tshombe, then prime minister of the Congo, to put down the rebellion, a number of African countries resented the action and the U.S. role in it. Francis Plimpton thought this caused support for the application of Article 19 to fall to less than two-thirds.[78]

Feeling that the showdown would come December 1 when the Assembly opened, Dick Pedersen and I proposed that the United States delay its contribution to the UN Special Fund and the Expanded Program of Technical Assistance instead of making a pledge November 16 at the scheduled pledging conference. This maneuver, which was then approved in Washington, was intended to signal that financial irresponsibility on peacekeeping could undermine confidence in the UN. It was a carefully limited risk, since we knew the contribution would not be needed or made until 1965, and it became pointless when the expected December 1 showdown did not materialize. The United States did in fact make its contribution early in 1965, in ample time to avoid damage to the two programs.

Stevenson had paid little attention to the financial problem until it became a political crisis in 1964. He was disturbed about the potential damage to the UN. On November 20 he arranged a meeting with Fedorenko to discuss ways of avoiding an Article 19 confrontation and the idea of a no-vote Assembly was brought up. Stevenson reported this idea favorably to Washington, and according to Beichman, this came as "a total surprise and shock to Washington officials." Beichman reports that Rusk agreed at breakfast the next morning and asks: "Could he have done anything else?"[79]

In my opinion, Rusk could have disagreed if he had felt strongly about the issue. Apparently he did not, and it was difficult to tell from USUN what all the factors in his decision were. We did know that Ambassador Llewellyn ("Tommie") Thompson was concerned about the effect a UN confrontation would have on Soviet-American relations.

I doubt that the United States could have had a showdown December 1 even if it had insisted on it; the majority of Third World countries appeared determined to avoid a confrontation. Chief Adebo, the Nigerian permanent representative, probably spoke for many when he said: "Nobody is prepared to blow up the World Organization on the altar of a principle founded upon Charter provisions of an admittedly ambiguous character."[80] David Kay observes:

Regardless of its substantive content, the question of the application of Article 19 was transformed into a direct United States–U.S.S.R. confrontation, with the very existence of the Organization at stake. Primarily responsible for this transformation of the constitutional question of the applicability of the provisions of Article 19 into a highly charged political question concerning the future of the Organization was the Soviet threat to leave the United Nations if Article 19 were invoked against it. In the face of this great power clash, the unity the new nations had demonstrated in 1963 dissolved, and these nations failed to take any decisive action designed to resolve the conflict. Faced with dissension within their ranks and a pervasive feeling of impotency over their own ability to affect the outcome of a direct great power collision, inaction and a willingness to agree to any subterfuge as long as it avoided this collision became the dominant themes of the political activity of the new nations at the abortive nineteenth session of the Assembly.[81]

Nevertheless, some of us at USUN would have preferred that the United States stand aside from any no-vote deal and wait to be persuaded not to press the issue on December 1. By hanging tough we might have induced Third World leaders to put greater pressure on the Soviet Union and France for contributions.

The General Assembly opened on December 1 and proceeded throughout the month without voting. This made little difference, since the first three or four weeks of any Assembly session are normally occupied by general debate while the real work of preparing resolutions and negotiating on them goes on privately. Where there were disagreements, the President of the Assembly, Alex Quaison-Sackey of Ghana, carried out a special "consultation" procedure in his office that amounted to an unofficial straw vote. He then stated to the General Assembly that a decision would be considered adopted if no objection were raised.

Meanwhile Quaison-Sackey and other representatives worked privately in efforts to resolve the crisis. The Afro-Asian states proposed a Rescue Fund to which all nations would make voluntary contributions. The Soviet Union, after protracted and laborious negotiations, told the Secretary General it would make a contribution but refused to specify the amount and date of payment, demanding in return that the Assembly resume normal business and voting procedures. The United States refused to accept this proposal, describing it as a "pig in a poke."

Before the Assembly resumed in February, Ralph Bunche, on behalf of the Secretary General, phoned Stevenson to suggest that the United States agree to let the nineteenth session proceed normally, including voting, with the understanding that the showdown would come in September. During USUN discussions I urged that we go along with this proposal, even though it was legally dubious. Having been in favor of a December 1, 1964 showdown, I had seen the erosion of Third World support for applying Article 19 during December and January and felt that it would continue. The only hope, as I saw it, was to say to the Third World countries: "Okay. You believe that this temporary suspension of the Charter provision (Article 19) will produce an adequate Soviet contribution. We'll go along, reluctantly, on the understanding that you and we together will insist that Article 19 be applied when the twentieth session opens in September if the delinquents [which by that time included France and ten other countries as well as the USSR] have not made adequate contributions by then." Politically, I felt, such a move would have aligned us with the majority and put the Soviet Union and France in a difficult position. Stevenson's other principal advisers disagreed, and Bunche's suggestion was rejected.

Bunche was a most remarkable man, the most influential American who ever served as the UN Secretariat. A graduate of UCLA and Ph.D. from Harvard, he was the principal writer of Gunnar Mydal's report on racism, *An American Dilemma*. He joined the UN Secretariat as Assistant Secretary General with responsibility for colonial issues. During the war of Israeli independence of 1948, he was assigned as deputy to Count Bernadotte in a mission to bring an end to the fighting and strive for peace. After Bernadotte was assassinated, Bunche took over the mission. Brilliant and indefatigable, he brought about truce agreements between Israel and the Arab combatants, Egypt, Syria, Lebanon, and Jordan, for which he was awarded the Nobel Peace Prize.

Bunche then became Undersecretary General for Special Political Affairs, the most important political post in the Secretariat. By agreement among the major powers, the post of Undersecretary General for Political and Security Affairs was reserved to the Soviet Union. It soon became clear that the Soviet occupants of the post were acting under instructions from Moscow. Understandably, the Secretary General was reluctant to rely on someone so instructed to carry out functions in an impartial way; hence, Dag Hammarskjöld created the post of Undersecretary General for Special Political Affairs. Bunche and Hammarskjöld worked together in creating the first peacekeeping force following the Arab-Israeli war of 1956. After that Bunche essentially ran peacekeeping operations until his retirement in 1971. He was most influential, not because he was an American but because his brilliance, hard work, and objectivity were recognized by the four secretaries general under whom he served and by the states members of the United Nations.

I had occasion to run up against his strict standards of integrity. A member of the Secretariat from Upper Volta (now Burkina Faso) was toying with a pistol in his office and accidentally shot off his finger. Bunche decided that, after such irresponsible conduct, he must be fired. A number of African delegates with whom I had friendly relations asked me to intervene with Bunche to get him to relent. Anxious to retain their goodwill, I did. Bunche proceeded to put me in my place, asking, "What business is this of yours?" He applied the same rules to everybody, regardless of race or nationality. Certainly not because of my intervention, perhaps because of African representatives, the official was not fired but transferred to Geneva.

When I retired from the Foreign Service and became a professor in the City University of New York (CUNY), I persuaded the President of the CUNY Graduate Center to establish an institute on the United Nations. At the suggestion of Dean Benjamin Rivlin, we named it the Ralph Bunche Institute on the United Nations. I was Director of the Institute for twelve years, after which Ben became the Director and I a Senior Fellow, my present position.

My unsuccessful intervention with Bunche illustrates another function of the U.S. mission to the UN. As representatives of the host country, we often dealt with problems of the other delegations.

On one occasion the ambassador of a West African country called us about his Cadillac, which had been stolen. The car was ten months old. Originally it had cost $10,000, but his insurance company was willing to pay only $6,000, their estimate of its current value as a used car. How could he explain to his government the need for an additional $4,000? We asked for the name of his insurance company and called them. Its president turned out to be a reputed Mafia boss. He was very accommodating and told us the ambassador would have an identical car the next morning—and he did! We wondered whose Cadillac might have been stolen that night but were pleased that we had been able to help the ambassador.

The General Assembly, having completed the bare essentials of its business—the budget and elections to fill vacancies—without voting, was getting ready to adjourn February 16. Then Halim Budo of Albania formally proposed that the Assembly proceed immediately on its normal work "in accordance with the Charter"—and asked for a decision by roll call vote. The President adjourned the meeting for two days for consultations. On February 18 he ruled there was a consensus against reconsidering the Assembly's previous decision not to vote. Budo challenged his ruling. Stevenson then stated to the Assembly that, so that the overwhelming majority might not be frustrated by one member, the United States would not object to one procedural vote, without prejudice to its position on the applicability of Article 19. Albania's motion lost, 2 (Albania, Mauritania) in favor, 97 against (including the USSR and the United States), and 13 abstentions.

Negotiations attempting to resolve the crisis continued during the spring. At USUN it became clear that a majority of countries would want to resume normal business when the twentieth session opened in September and that the pressure would now be on the United States rather than on the delinquents. There also appeared to be a weakening of ardor in Washington where some officials became concerned that enforcement of Article 19 against the USSR and France might create a precedent by which the Assembly could create a UN Capital Development Fund—which the United States opposed—and assess the United States for one-third of its resources. There was also concern that an Assembly majority might someday launch a peacekeeping operation that the United States opposed. Nevertheless, at USUN the prevailing view, in which Stevenson concurred wholeheartedly, was that something should be done to resolve the financial crisis and thus strengthen the UN. We proposed that, at the San Francisco ceremony in June 1965 celebrating the UN's twentieth anniversary, President Johnson would announce American willingness to contribute $25 million to a Rescue Fund provided the Soviets contributed a similar amount. (The Soviet contribution would be in new funds and enough to take them out of the reach of Article 19, whereas the U.S. contribution would be largely in the cancellation of debts owed to us by the UN for logistical help in the Congo and certain "surplus accounts," none of which would be collectible unless the deficit was resolved.) Such an offer would have vastly improved the U.S. political position at the UN and put great pressure on the Soviets and French to contribute. State accepted the idea, and Stevenson, with staff help, prepared a draft for Johnson. Unfortunately, there was a leak to the press, which State Department insiders attribute to Harlan Cleveland. Two days before the San Francisco ceremony James Reston wrote a column in the *New York Times* predicting that Johnson would announce a compromise. Thereupon Johnson, who hated to be scooped, had the speech rewritten in Washington, completely eliminating any U.S. offer. As a result, the "celebration" in San Francisco seemed more like a dirge. (There is no evidence that Johnson had either accepted or rejected the idea of a $25 million contribution; what is certain is that the leak to Reston killed any chance the idea had ever had.)

After that it was clear that a majority could not be mustered to enforce Article 19 and that the USSR and France would make no contribution by September to make the question moot. Arthur Goldberg's statement on August 16 broke the voting deadlock (see Chapter IX); however, the authority of the General Assembly had been substantially weakened, along with the financial situation of the UN.

A number of writers have criticized the United States for its efforts to have Article 19 enforced. H.G. Nicolas, for example, writes:

It was the U.S. that embarked in the mid-sixties upon the vain and harmful exercises connected with the invocation of Article 17 and 19, which reduced the organization to the most degrading level of impotence. And this was an adventure which had its inception entirely in a belief that the Charter was some kind of timeless, self-enforcing prescription, whose wording could be construed without reference to the politics of the membership.[82]

Ruth Russell also criticizes the United States for becoming obsessed by legalistic arguments; she contrasts the American refusal to contribute to the Rescue Fund with the attitude of Great Britain, which contributed $10 million, Canada ($4 million), Japan, and the Nordic countries. These states had also paid their assessments, as had the United States; however, they chose to put belief in a stronger UN above arguments about legal responsibility.[83] A U.S. offer of $25 million, as advocated by USUN, would have helped substantially to put the UN on a sounder financial footing and put great pressure on the Soviets and French to match it. Unfortunately, Stevenson did not have enough influence on Johnson to maintain the offer after the press leak.

The real loss, however, was not to the United States so much as it was to the UN and the smaller and medium-sized states that make up its majority. Their votes dominate the General Assembly, and their backdown on Article 19 meant that any major power, and other states as well, could defy the assessment power of the Assembly, one of its few real powers under the Charter. Indeed, given present moods of the Assembly majority, this "loss" may now seem comforting to Washington. As Stoessinger put it, the Article 19 controversy was really a conflict between those who wanted to maintain the United Nations as "static conference machinery" (the USSR and Gaullist France) and those who wished to endow it with increasing strength and executive authority.[84] Now it is the United States that is delinquent in its payment of UN assessments to a degree that is seriously harmful to the functioning of the UN.

THE UN DEVELOPMENT DECADE

On the economic side, the United States continued to give strong support to the UN throughout Stevenson's tenure, although Stevenson himself took only a sporadic interest in anything nonpolitical. He was enthusiastically supportive of the work done by Klutznick and me on economic issues and enjoyed making the principal U.S. statement in Geneva when the Economic and Social Council met there each summer (which also gave him an opportunity to take a brief vacation in Europe); however, in New York it was impossible to get his sustained attention on economic or financial issues.

Early in the Kennedy administration (1961) Richard Gardner, then Deputy Assistant Secretary of State for International Organization affairs, phoned me from Washington and read a proposal for a UN Development Decade. He, Harlan Cleveland, and other Kennedy New Frontiersmen were strongly supportive of the UN and eager to demonstrate the new administration's interest. Their first idea was an International Development Year; however, the Treasury department was concerned that designating a single year would bring pressure for more financial aid. It was then decided to propose a Development Decade, which emphasized aspects of development other than quantities of aid: for example, intensified international cooperation, better coordination, improved adaptation of science and technology, and better development planning.

I told Gardner that the ideas were all laudable but that they had already been put forward by the United States in 1958, in what was called at USUN the "Charting Anew" resolution.[85] He replied that the principles might have been similar but the follow-through would be different, as the Kennedy administration was different from Eisenhower's. In fact, he and Harlan Cleveland labored mightily to make it so, and there were some constructive achievements even though the original proposal had little in the way of concrete commitments.[86]

Addressing the General Assembly on September 25, 1961, President Kennedy launched the proposal with the following brief reference:

Political sovereignty is but a mockery without the means of meeting poverty and illiteracy and disease. Self-determination is but a slogan if the future holds no hope.

That is why my nation—which has freely shared its capital and its technology to help others help themselves—now proposes officially designating this decade of the 1960s as the United Nations Decade of Development. Under the framework of that resolution the United Nations' existing efforts in promoting economic growth can be expanded and coordinated. Regional surveys and training institutes can now pool the talents of many. New research, technical assistance, and pilot projects can unlock the wealth of less developed lands and untapped waters. And development can become a cooperative and not a competitive enterprise—to enable all nations, however diverse in their systems and beliefs, to become in fact as well as in law both free and equal nations.[87]

The delegation then began consultations with a view to gathering a representative group of cosponsors in the Second (Economic) Committee, where the item would be considered. The objective was to have one or two cosponsors from each geographic area but to avoid having such a large group of cosponsors as to make the consideration of proposed amendments too complicated.

Because Phil Klutznick, our ECOSOC representative, was completely absorbed in getting the UN bond issue through the Fifth Committee, the responsibility for gaining Second Committee approval of the Decade of Development was almost entirely mine. Friends cultivated there during my previous four sessions, particularly among the Asian and African delegations, were most helpful in gaining support. Candor also seemed to help. In a private meeting, when the Indonesian and other Third World representatives asked what was new and concrete in the proposal, I answered frankly that there was nothing specific but that they would be unwise to reject the first offer from a new American President. The terms of the resolution were broad and positive; they had nothing to lose by accepting it and using it as a basis for concrete negotiations. In the end, that is what they did.

One problem of status was that the Indian prime minister had proposed to the General Assembly an International Cooperation Year. We accommodated the Indian delegation by entitling the resolution: "The United National Development Decade: A Programme for International Economic Cooperation."

We had another problem when one of the communist countries proposed an amendment by which the goal of the decade would have been to close the gap in income per capita between the developed and the less developed countries. Some of our cosponsors from less developed countries, in the sponsors' caucus, urged that we accept the amendment lest the resolution be lost. I argued that such a goal was clearly impossible and that we should not adopt language patently dishonest even to stave off a demagogic amendment. Instead, we stuck with a preambular clause reading as follows:

Noting, however that in spite of the efforts made in recent years the gap in *per capita* incomes between the economically developed and the less developed countries has increased and the rate of economic and social progress in the developing countries is still far from adequate.

We did, however, accept another very significant amendment in the key paragraph of the resolution, setting a quantitative target for growth in national income. This involved a struggle with Washington, where the Treasury Department was reluctant to see any quantitative goals specified, fearing that these would be translated into demands for more financial aid. As amended and adopted, the paragraph read:

1. *Designates* the current decade as the United Nations Development Decade, in which Member States and their peoples will intensify their efforts to mobilize and to sustain support for the measures required on the part of both developed and developing countries to accelerate progress towards self-sustaining growth of the economy of the individual nations and their social advancement so as to attain in each under-developed country a substantial increase in the rate of growth, with each country setting its own target, taking as the objective a minimum annual rate of growth of aggregate national income of 5 percent at the end of the Decade.[88]

Ironically, the 5 percent goal was attained, and this was the feature of the decade—accepted reluctantly by Washington—to which the United States pointed with greatest pride in 1970.

The rest of the resolution was a list of general principles of conduct that would contribute to the goal set forth in paragraph 1: for example, stabilization of prices for primary commodities; a fair share of earnings from the extraction and marketing of natural resources; increased flow of private capital; help in working out economic development plans; accelerating the elimination of illiteracy, hunger, and disease; improved education and vocational training; intensified research; and opening markets to the manufactured goods of the less developed countries. These principles had been largely accepted before 1961, and the full implementation of them remained a target in 2000. However, linking them together in one resolution, together with the 5 percent growth target, provided a rallying point for the less developed countries, and its unanimous adoption was a public relations triumph for the new Kennedy administration. It also provided the heads of specialized agencies such as the FAO, WHO, ILO, and UNESCO with reasons for projecting increased budgets. Also, in a companion resolution, the General Assembly raised the target of the Expanded Program of Technical Assistance and the Special Fund to a combined total of $150 million.[89] It had first been $100 million and by 1979 was over $600 million for the combined program, now known as the UN Development Program. There was also a substantial increase in financial aid during the first half of the decade, for which a good part of the credit should go to the Development Assistance Committee of the OECD; its member governments; and the

World Bank and its new soft-loan affiliate, the International Development Association.[90]

Even so, the resolution would never have come through unanimously and so close to the original American design if the Soviet representative, Lavrichenko, had not been so disagreeable and inept. His vehement and often unfounded attacks against the United States and the resolution created a lot of sympathy for us. At a luncheon following one of Lavrichenko's tirades, Hector Bernardo of Argentina showed me two pages of troublesome amendments he had planned to propose, then ripped them up, telling all of us that this represented his response to Lavrichenko. During one of Lavrichenko's tirades, I slipped our United Kingdom neighbor a note saying, "I think this guy is being paid by the CIA." He wrote back, "This would be one of the few times they got their money's worth."

Stevenson was delighted with the unanimous vote for the Development Decade and was aware of my role in achieving it. He told Klutznick to find out whether there was anything I wanted to keep me happy in my job. I was pleased with Stevenson's appreciation, but did not ask for anything.

In fact, I had achieved considerable influence with the other members of the Second (Economic) Committee. Being the representative of the United States gave my position importance. Beyond that, I had cultivated good relationships with representatives of countries on all parts of the political spectrum. I never lied, deceived, or broke faith with anyone. I was always well informed on the issues. I was friendly and available to anyone who wanted to negotiate or consult. One leftist representative gave me his book and inscribed it to "the ever popular representative of unpopular causes." These personal factors do make a difference, above all a reputation for integrity. Once that is lost, a diplomat is useless or worse, particularly at the UN, which is a glass house in more ways than one.

Individuals and relationships do make a difference. Once, when I was lobbying a Central American representative for a vote, he said, "Look, just tell me what you want, and if it's not coffee or bananas, I'll go along." As this comment indicates a representative will not vote against his country's vital interests, but there are many situations where such interests are not involved, and in those cases, the ability to win and keep friends is important.

THE UN INSTITUTE FOR TRAINING AND RESEARCH (UNITAR)

In 1963, Harlan Cleveland received the impression that the Ford Foundation, with assets booming along with the stock market, could be prepared to give $2 million toward the establishment of a United Nations Institute to serve as a "think tank" for the Secretary General. It turned out to be an illusion that gave rise to an institution.

Cleveland's deputy, Dick Gardner, sketched out plans for the institute and prepared a draft resolution for the General Assembly. Then Dick and I discussed broad outlines and tactics. The Ford Foundation would want Assembly approval, matching contributions from government and private sources, and assurances of a high-quality institute of the Rand Corporation type. The secretary general and his top associates are too much immersed in day-to-day business to do long-range planning and research in depth on problems that confront the organization, both in keeping the peace and in promoting economic development. Moreover, actual or potential Secretariat officials, particularly those from the new countries, could profit from specialized preservice or inservice training. These were the broad aims of the UN Training and Research Institute as we envisaged it. (The name was later changed to United Nations Institute for Training and Research, so as to provide a more felicitous acronym.)

For tactical reasons I suggested we ask that the question be discussed in the Second (Economic) Committee, where our network of friends was strong. Since the institute would have peace and security as well as economic and social aspects, it could have gone to the First Committee or the Special Political Committee if we had considered either of those forums as favorable. Also, I asked Nonnie Wright, the veteran and very popular Danish representative in the Second Committee, whether she would take the leadership of the proposal in the committee. She readily agreed and rounded up a representative group of sixteen cosponsors. The United States joined as the seventeenth cosponsor after the resolution was well along its way to approval in the committee. (This was the same Nonnie Wright who in 1958 had successfully initiated a campaign to name Paul Hoffman as managing director of the Special Fund, when the U.S. candidate was someone else.)

In committee the Soviets opposed the idea of an institute because it was a Western idea and designed to strengthen the role of the secretary general. The French were wary of it because they, too, did not want to see the role of the secretary general enhanced. Nevertheless, the resolution was approved by an overwhelming majority, including virtually all Third World countries.

Next came the problem of raising funds. Thant strongly favored the proposal. To help in getting contributions, he wanted a brochure describing briefly the aims and proposed structure of the new institute. Paul Hoffman, for whom I had done some drafting when he was U.S. delegate to the Second Committee in 1956, suggested to Thant that he enlist my services. Thant then asked Stevenson to lend me to the Secretariat to work on the brochure. Stevenson agreed to second me, as a result of which I worked on the project from Christmas through New Year's Day.

My draft was discussed with Thant's principal aides, who made suggestions. The most significant one came from Ralph Bunche, who, as the official principally responsible for the UN's peacekeeping operations, did not want the term "peacekeeping" used as a topic of institute concern. We then substituted the phrase "UN operations in troubled areas." I also consulted at various stages with a key official at the Ford Foundation, in order to be sure we did nothing to offend an institution that was expected to contribute about half of the funds.

Thant then asked the UN High Commissioner for Refugees to second his fund-raiser, Peter Casson, and the commissioner agreed. Casson, astute, persistent, and indefatigable, succeeded in raising $2.6 million in contributions and pledges from outside the United States. Then came the big surprise. The Ford Foundation rejected the Secretary General's request for a founding contribution, though it expressed its willingness to consider requests for aid on individual projects on their merits.

The project had by that time gathered its own momentum, even though the assumption on which it was initiated proved to be unfounded. Thant and Casson persuaded John D. Rockefeller III to buy for $500,000 a five-story building on Forty-fifth Street and United Nations Plaza, facing the UN, and donate it as the headquarters for the institute. Moreover, the U.S. government, observing how many other governments had contributed, came up with $400,000 for the institute plus $100,000 for Adlai Stevenson Fellowships to be used for trainees from the new countries. Stevenson had died a year earlier, and the fellowship program was an appropriate memorial.

Unfortunately, UNITAR's problems were more than financial. To gain the confidence of leading foundations and universities, an executive director of outstanding reputation would have been required. Instead, the secretary general decided to make his choice on a political basis; this became clear when Dick Gardner and I went to see Thant's *chef de cabinet*, C.V. Narasimhan. Dick suggested John Holmes, head of the Canadian Institute of International Affairs. Narasimhan did not comment on Holmes's qualifications but stated flatly that the executive director could not come from a NATO country. Looking at his constellation of undersecretaries general, Thant decided that he should have a French-speaking African at that level in order to obtain a better geopolitical balance. He chose Gabriel d'Arboussier, a distinguished, charming, and intelligent Senegalese. Unfortunately, d'Arboussier had no standing with the Western foundations where most of the potential nongovernmental sources of support lay, nor with the leading academic circles.

UNITAR has not become a Rand type of organization for the secretary general. It has, however, done commendable studies of economic and social issues and of the problems of negotiation, mediation, and the peaceful settlement of disputes. It has also performed an important training function.

CONCLUDING THOUGHTS

Measured against his stature in the nation and the world and his own expectations, Stevenson's term as permanent representative could be considered a failure. He was not in the President's inner circle for policy making. He was not on close terms with Secretary Rusk, with whom there was an underlying tension. His many other responsibilities and interests made him only a half-time representative. His reputation as an idealist gave him little clout on policy in the Kennedy and Johnson administrations, where the emphasis lay on being tough and practical. Moreover, his own nagging self-doubts made him appear indecisive and handicapped him severely in policy disputes with the bright, self-assured men who counseled the two presidents—Bundy, McNamara, and Rostow; they also had the advantage of being there, in Washington, full-time. Finally, feeling deep frustration at his inability to move U.S. policy on major world issues, he exhausted himself by working and playing too hard and consequently lost some of his zest and effectiveness.

Yet Stevenson did a laudable job of representing the United States at the UN. His very presence was recognized as a sign that the United States attached importance to the organization. He assembled a distinguished and capable staff of top deputies. As we have noted, he had public presence, wit, an original mind, and great skills as a diplomat and orator. He was respected not only among Western delegates but also among those of the Third World as a distinguished, decent man who believed deeply in peace and justice. He was also superb in building support for the UN among the American people.

The tragedy was that Stevenson did not have more impact on the policies of Kennedy and Johnson. In retrospect, his doubts on escalating the war in Vietnam appear far wiser than the decisions of those bright, self-assured men whose counsels prevailed.

NOTES

1. Kenneth S. Davis, *The Politics of Honor: A Biography of Adlai E. Stevenson* (New York: Putnam, 1967), pp. 404–5.
2. Theodore Sorenson, *Kennedy* (New York: Harper & Row, 1965), p. 254.
3. Stevenson served most effectively and with great distinction as U.S. Delegation Press Relations chief, when the UN Charter was completed at San Francisco in 1945; as replacement for Edward Stettinius, U.S. Representative to the Preparatory Commission at London in 1946; and as Senior Adviser to the U.S. Delegation to the First Session of the UN General Assembly. He had hoped to become Permanent Representative in 1946, but the job went to Austin; he was, however, Alternate Delegate to the UN General Assembly in 1946 and 1947. See Bert Cochran,

Adlai Stevenson—Patrician among Politicians (New York: Funk & Wagnalls, 1969), pp. 140–45. Also, John B. Martin, *Adlai Stevenson and the World* (New York: Doubleday, 1977), pp. 556–65, describes Stevenson's hesitation and dickering with Kennedy.

4. Arthur M. Schlesinger, Jr., *A Thousand Days: John F. Kennedy in the White House* (Boston: Houghton Mifflin, 1965), pp. 462–66. See also Martin, *Adlai Stevenson and the World*, pp. 586–87.

5. Schlesinger, *A Thousand Days*, p. 462.

6. Martin, 581–87. See also Arnold Beichman, *The "Other" State Department* (New York: Basic Books, 1967), pp. 145–46. See also Martin, *Adlai Stevenson and the World*, pp. 581–657.

7. Richard Walton, *The Remnants of Power* (New York: Coward-McCann 1968), p. 26. Davis *The Politics of Honor* (p. 459) reports that he was not consulted nor even adequately informed of important policy development with whose issue he disagreed personally but must defend before the U.N.

8. Martin (p. 650) quotes Stevenson as saying in a letter to Hubert Humphrey: "I feel that when he wants my point of view he will ask for it."

9. Martin, *Adlai Stevenson and the World*, p. 707 (II).

10. See John B. Martin, *Adlai Stevenson of Illinois* (Garden City, N.Y.: Doubleday, 1976) (I).

11. Ibid.

12. Cochran, *Adlai Stevenson*, p. 198.

13. Martin, *Adlai Stevenson of Illinois*, p. 693; and Davis, p. 421.

14. Walton, *The Remnants of Power*, pp. 212–17, describes the institutional problems that inhibited Stevenson's influence on policy. Cochran, *Adlai Stevenson*, p. 318, concludes that Stevenson's influence on shaping policy was neglible; that is, he had "prestige without power."

15. Martin, *Adlai Stevenson and the World*, p. 761.

16. Ibid., pp. 747–48.

17. USUN telegram 851, September 21, 1962. A sanitized version is available in the Kennedy Library, Boston: NSF: Portugal 9/1/62–9/28/62, Box 154.

18. Cochran, *Adlai Stevenson*, p. 336.

19. Martin, *Adlai Stevenson and the World*, p. 590.

20. Ibid., p. 591.

21. Ernest W. Lefever, *Crisis in the Congo* (Washington, D.C.: Brookings Institution, 1965), p. 51.

22. S. C. Res. S/4741, February 21, 1961. Text reproduced in Lefever, *Crisis in the Congo*, p. 193.

23. Schlesinger, *A Thousand Days*, p. 575.

24. UN Security Council, *Official Records*, 943d meeting, February 15, 1961. See also Martin, *Adlai Stevenson and the World*, pp. 610–13.

25. Roger Hilsman, *The Politics of Policy Making in Defense and Foreign Affairs* (New York: Harper & Row), 1988.

26. Ibid., pp. 250–71. See also Lefever, *Crisis in the Congo*, Chap. 3 and 4. As Lefever indicates, casualties were high, pp. 113–14.

27. The only notable action by the Council was its adoption on November 24, 1961, by a vote of 9 to 0 (France and Britain abstaining), of resolution S/5002, which in paragraph 4 authorized the secretary general "to take vigorous action,

including the use of a requisite measure of force, if necessary, for the immediate apprehension, detention pending legal action and/or deportation of all foreign military and para-military personnel and political advisers not under the United Nations Command, and mercenaries." This provision was intended to strengthen the secretary general's hand in dealing with the Katanga secession, and it did.

28. Lefever, *Crisis in the Congo*, p. 120. Conor Cruise O'Brien, who was the UN representative in Katanga from June to November 1961, charges that Hammarskjöld bent to British pressure in September when UN troops used force in an operation aimed at ending Tshombe's secession. The UN's official report on the violence of September 13, described UN troops as responding to attacks by the Katangese gendarmerie. O'Brien felt that this evasive and, in his view, distorted account encouraged the Tshombe regime to continue its secession, whereas a forthright UN campaign to end the secession by force would have succeeded quickly. It is difficult to judge the correctness of O'Brien's estimate of success. On the other hand, it is an established principle of UN peacekeeping operations that force is to be used only in self-defense, not for offensive operations. Even though the Security Council's resolution of February 21, 1961 authorized "the use of force, if necessary, in the last resort," this was to be done only "to prevent the occurrence of civil war in the Congo." Given the European, especially British, outcry against the operation and the principle that UN peacekeeping units use force only in self-defense, it is understandable that Hammarskjöld's official version emphasized self-defense. See Conor Cruise O'Brien, *To Katanga and Back* (New York: Simon & Schuster, 1962), pp. 219–88.

29. Ibid., p. 62.

30. O'Brien, *To Katanga and Back*, pp. 40–67, alleges that three top Americans in the Secretariat—Cordier, Bunche, and Weischoff—actually formed the inner circle of Hammarskjöld's advisers. He does not challenge their loyalty to Hammarskjöld or the UN but argues that their cultural background necessarily influenced their viewpoints, a valid point. Weischoff died with Hammarskjöld in the plane crash of September 1961, and Cordier retired shortly thereafter. Bunche continued as U Thant's top adviser on peacekeeping until the end of ONUC in 1964, but he was a man of very independent mind. To my personal knowledge, he stubbornly and successfully resisted U.S. pressure to extend ONUC beyond June 1964 and never hesitated to disagree with Washington or Stevenson on other issues if his independent mind so indicated.

31. Schlesinger, *A Thousand Days*, p. 271.

32. Ibid., pp. 271–73.

33. Ibid., pp. 484–86.

34. The members of the Executive Committee were: Dean Rusk, Secretary of State; Robert McNamara, Secretary of Defense; Robert F. Kennedy, Attorney General; John McCone, Director of the CIA; Douglas Dillon, Secretary of the Treasury; McGeorge Bundy, Adviser on National Security Affairs; Theodore Sorenson, Presidential Counsel; George Ball, Undersecretary of State; U. Alexis Johnson, Deputy Undersecretary of State; General Maxwell Taylor, Chairman of the Joint Chiefs of Staff; Edward Martin, Assistant Secretary of State for Latin American Affairs; Llewellyn Thompson, Adviser on Soviet Affairs; Rosewell Gilpatric, Deputy Secretary of Defense; Paul Nitze, Assistant Secretary of Defense. Intermittently: Lyndon B. Johnson, Vice President; Ambassador Adlai Stevenson; Ken O'Donnell, Special

Assistant to the President; Dan Wilson, Deputy Director, USIA. For a full account of its deliberations, see Robert F. Kennedy, *Thirteen Days* (New York: Norton, 1969).

35. Walton, *The Remnants of Power*, p. 40.
36. Schlesinger, *A Thousand Days*, pp. 810–11. In my interview (October 31, 1977) with Richard Pedersen, who had been senior political adviser in 1962, he told me that he and Charles Yost had worked with Stevenson in preparing this negotiating position.
37. Adlai E. Stevenson, *Looking Outward*, ed. Robert Schiffer and Selma Schiffer (New York: Harper & Row, 1963), pp. 97–98.
38. See ibid., pp. 79–112, for text of Stevenson speeches and his exchange with Zorin wherein he challenged the Soviet representatives to deny that there was offensive Soviet missiles in Cuba and said he was prepared to wait for the reply "until Hell freezes over." See also Davis, *The Politics of Honor*, pp. 482–85.
39. Stevenson, *Looking Outward*, pp. 125–28.
40. Ruth B. Russell, *The United Nations and United States Security Policy* (Washington, DC: Brookings Instuition, 1968), p. 76.
41. Cochran, *Adlai Stevenson*, pp. 324–25. It should be noted that Stevenson put forward his negotiating suggestions during a brainstorming session of the Executive Committee when all possibilities were being explored and he concurred fully with the Executive Committee's decision. Dean Rusk said: "The mix that turned out had a good Stevenson output in it. It was a place where his influence was significant. We were all doves and hawks trying to find an alternative to force." Quoted in Walton, *The Remnants of Power*, p. 65. See also Beichman, *The "Other" State Department*, pp. 146–48; Martin, *Adlai Stevenson and the World*, pp. 722–23.
42. Cochran, *Adlai Stevenson*, p. 318.
43. Martin, *Adlai Stevensoon and the World*, p. 684.
44. Ibid., p. 782; and Davis, *The Politics of Honor*, pp. 488–90.
45. Lyndon B. Johnson, *The Vantage Point: Perspectives of the Presidency 1963–69* (New York: Holt, Rinehart, Winston, 1970), pp. 611–12, 667–69.
46. Martin, *Adlai Stevenson and the World*, pp. 827–28.
47. Walton, *The Remnants of Power*, pp. 141–42; and Davis, *The Politics of Honor*, pp. 494–98.
48. Walton, *The Remnants of Power*, pp. 144–45.
49. Martin, *Adlai Stevenson and the World*, p. 811.
50. Ibid., pp. 840–41.
51. Ibid., pp. 830–31.
52. Davis, *The Politics of Honor*, pp. 501–3; Cochran, *Adlai Stevenson*, pp. 328–29; and Martin, *Adlai Stevenson and the World*, pp. 857–59.
53. Martin, *Adlai Stevenson and the World*, p. 861. See also Johnson, op. cit., pp. 781–82, 798–99, and 839 for evidence that Stevenson did not oppose "containment" in Vietnam.
54. Martin, *Adlai Stevenson and the World*, p. 856.
55. Quoted in Johnson, *The Vantage Point*, p. 757.
56. Cochran, *Adlai Stevenson*, pp. 326–28.
57. U Thant address, May 27, 1965, in *UN Monthly Chronicle* 2 (June 1965); p. 69.

58. Thomas Franck and Edward Weisband, *Word Politics: Verbal Strategy among the Superpowers* (New York: Oxford University Press, 1971). For a description and analysis of the Brezhnev doctrine and its implications, see Ivo Duchacek, *Nations and Men*, 3d ed. (Hinsdale, Ill.: Dryden, 1975), pp. 424–26.

59. UN Security Council, Official Records, May 3, 1965. See also Martin, *Adlai Stevenson and the World*, pp. 843–47. The United States also argued that the action was an exercise of self-defense, invoking the January 1962 Declaration of Punta del Este, which had declared Marxism-Leninism incompatible with the Inter-American system and had urged OAS members: "to take those steps that they may consider appropriate for their individual or collective self-defense, and to cooperate, as may be necessary or desirable, to strengthen their capacity to counteract threats or acts of aggression, subversion, or other dangers to peace and security resulting from the continued intervention in this hemisphere of Sino-Soviet powers, in accordance with the obligations established in treaties and agreements . . . such as the OAS Charter and the Rio Treaty." Leonard C. Meeker, address before Foreign Law Association, U.S. Department of State, *Bulletin* 53 (1965); p. 62.

60. S. C. Res. 203, May 14, 1965.

61. UN press release M-1709, December 31, 1966, p. 7.

62. Walt W. Rostow, *The Diffusion of Power* (New York: Macmillan, 1972), p. 415.

63. Martin, *Adlai Stevenson and the World*, p. 844.

64. Ibid., pp. 860–61.

65. U Thant, address May 27, 1965, in *UN Monthly Chronicle* 2 (June 1965), pp. 361–76.

66. G. A. Res. 1619 (XV), April 21, 1961. The vote was 54 (including the United States, the United Kingdom, Canada, the Nordic Countries, and 21 new nations) to 15 (including the Soviet bloc), with 23 abstentions.

67. Letter dated December 1, 1977, from Philip M. Klutznick to the author.

68. U Thant, address May 27, 1965, in *UN Monthly Chronicle* 2 (June 1965), 85–91.

69. G. A. Res. 1739 (XVI), December 20, 1961. The vote was 58 to 13 (France, Belgium, and 11 communist states), with 24 abstentions.

70. Letter to the author from Klutznick, December 1, 1977.

71. John G. Stoessinger, *The United Nations and the Superpowers* (New York: Random House, 1965), pp. 98–102.

72. ICJ Reports, 1962, pp. 151, 179–80.

73. G. A. Res. 1854(XVII), December 19, 1962.

74. Soviet memorandum.

75. Beichman, *The "Other" State Department*, pp. 149–53.

76. Walton, *The Remnants of Power*, p. 87.

77. See U.S. State Department, *Article 19 of the Charter of the United Nations: Memorandum of Law*, Washington, DC, 1964. Note also that on Jan. 2, 1980, Sudan was informed by the UN Secretariat that it had lost its right to vote under Article 19, this without General Assembly action, *New York Times*, January 17, 1980, p. A-9, col. 1.

78. Walton, *The Remnants of Power*, pp. 87–91.

79. Beichman, *The "Other" State Department*, pp. 155, 163.

80. UN General Assembly, *Official Records*, A/C.121, April 29, 1965, p. 5.

81. David Kay, *The New Nations in the United Nations* (New York: Columbia University Press, 1970), p. 129.

82. H. G. Nicholas, *The United Nations as a Political Institution*, 4th ed. (London: Oxford University Press, 1971), p. 264.

83. Russell, *The United Nations*, pp. 440–43.

84. Stoessinger, *The United Nations and the Superpowers*, p. 110.

85. G. A. Res. 1316 (XIII), December 12, 1958.

86. The achievements are described in Richard N. Gardner, *In Pursuit of World Order* (New York: Praeger, 1974), pp. 124–40.

87. Statement by President John F. Kennedy to the UN General Assembly, September 25, 1961.

88. G. A. Res. 1710 (XVI), December 19, 1961.

89. G. A. Res. 715 (XVI), December 19, 1961.

90. Gardner, *In Pursuit of World Order*, pp. 126–31.

CHAPTER IX

Arthur J. Goldberg: A Justice Comes to the UN

Arthur Goldberg arrived at USUN with a strong mandate. He came as "the representative of Lyndon Johnson,"[1] who had persuaded him to leave a lifetime job in the Supreme Court. Johnson referred to him as "an old and trusted friend of mine" and "a counselor of many years," who would sit in the cabinet and would "always have direct and ready access to, and the full and respectful confidence of, the President of the United States and the Secretary of State." Johnson added: "In his new office, he will speak not only for an administration, but will speak for the entire nation."[2]

The fact that Johnson sought Goldberg strengthened the new permanent representative's position, at least initially. The President called Goldberg on July 16, 1965, shortly after Adlai Stevenson's death, and said that he needed "an outstanding American to deal with the crisis at the UN" and to guide him to an early settlement of the Vietnam War. After another phone call from the President, Goldberg went to see him at the White House. While waiting in the anteroom, Goldberg was approached by a presidential assistant, Jack Valenti, who inquired whether he might not also be interested in the post of Secretary of the Department of Health, Education, and Welfare (HEW). Goldberg, with typical sensitivity, resented being treated like a job applicant, having come because the President had invited him to discuss the UN post. He told Valenti: "I'm not an applicant for any post—including the UN one." The President, who must have had some indication from Valenti of Goldberg's reaction to the HEW post, never mentioned it; instead, Johnson reemphasized how much the nation needed a man of Goldberg's stature at the UN. Goldberg again deferred his decision.

Shortly thereafter, Johnson asked Goldberg to accompany him to Bloomington, Illinois, for Adlai Stevenson's funeral, and on the plane coming back to Washington they had a long conversation. Goldberg told Johnson that leaving the Court would be a grave step and that he would need assurance before finally deciding on acceptance, not only that the UN ambassadorship would be elevated in general foreign policy making, but that he would be a principal advisor and participant in all decision making leading to a negotiated peace in Vietnam. He asked Johnson whether he was committed to such a peace. The President replied that he was and that one of his basic reasons for asking Goldberg to assume the UN post was to get the benefit of "America's greatest negotiator in reaching a peaceful solution; and soon."[3] (Another strong reason, and probably the principal one, which became evident later, was Johnson's desire to create a Supreme Court vacancy for his old friend Abe Fortas. Goldberg was aware that Fortas might be chosen but thought at the time that Fortas would be a good appointment.)

The weekend before Goldberg resigned from the Court he and his wife were guests at Camp David. That same weekend Secretary of Defense McNamara presented a proposal for calling up the Reserves for service in Vietnam. Goldberg told Johnson that if this were done he would withdraw his acceptance of the UN post because, to him, calling up the Reserves meant the equivalent of a formal declaration of war. Johnson did not give the order.[4] Still, Goldberg was aware of Johnson's plans for a massive increase in U.S. forces in Vietnam. Upon arriving at USUN in July 1965, he told some of us in private that the publicly announced increment that month, from 75,000 to 125,000, was only a beginning; by the end of 1966 there would be over 400,000 American troops in Vietnam. And there were.

Goldberg had valid reasons for insisting on a clear mandate before accepting the UN post. His seat on the Supreme Court was the most revered position in the law and a lifetime appointment of the olympian heights that included generous pensions for himself and his wife. He would be trading these for a hectic, backbreaking job in the hurly-burly of UN politics where he would serve at the President's pleasure. Yet he was intrigued by the new post. He had great, perhaps exaggerated, respect for the potential of the UN in "the effort to bring the rule of law to govern the relations between sovereign states. It is that or doom—and we all know it."[5] He observed that "in one generation the UN has created more international law than in all previous generations in man's history."[6] Shortly thereafter he said, "I consider the role of the U.S. Representative to the United Nations to be a dual one. He, of course, first represents the President of our government at the United Nations, but second, he also represents the United Nations to the American people."[7]

Another factor, as noted above, was Goldberg's sincere conviction that his efforts at the UN and in cabinet meetings could help to end the war in Vietnam. Having been at USUN for nine years when Goldberg arrived and having witnessed Stevenson's frustration, I was privately skeptical from the beginning about the extent to which the chief of our mission could have an impact. Hanoi, the Soviets, and the French did not want a UN role. When, in January 1966, the United States did attempt to get UN Security Council action on the issue, we managed with great effort to get the bare nine votes (out of fifteen) required for inscription of the item. The ninth vote (Japan) was conditioned on the understanding that the Council would not actually meet on this item until private consultations indicated that a meeting would be constructive—which never happened. The one point of agreement among the Council members was that the 1954 Geneva accords should be the basis of any new settlement.

Goldberg's efforts were not helped by the fact that the United States resumed the bombing of North Vietnam shortly after it requested Security Council consideration. According to Norman Cousins, the resumption of bombing on January 30, 1966 also derailed a meeting Cousins was to have with a Hanoi representative in Warsaw in February. Another meeting of Washington and Hanoi representatives in Warsaw envisaged for late 1966 was also aborted because of escalated U.S. bombings on the eve of scheduled meetings.[8] Small wonder that Goldberg's efforts at the UN were doomed to frustration.

Another clue to Goldberg's frustration on Vietnam is provided in Walt Rostow's book, *The Diffusion of Power*. Rostow described Johnson's national security policy as one built initially around Rusk, McNamara, and Bundy. Goldberg is mentioned as one who came "occasionally" to the Tuesday luncheons where crucial policy discussions took place. He suffered from an inherent handicap in having to be in New York most of the time, even though he did attend the formal National Security Council sessions regularly and worked superhuman hours to be in Washington for a policy role there while doing a superb job of running USUN. As Rostow was so close to the President, it is a significant indication of Rostow's attitude toward the UN that his lengthy book, covering more than a decade of foreign policy starting in 1958, makes only this one reference to Goldberg in his capacity of permanent representative in the UN. There is no reference whatsoever to other occupants of the post during the period covered—Lodge, Ball, Wiggins, Yost, and Scali. Lodge is mentioned only as Ambassador to Vietnam, Ball as Undersecretary of State, and Goldberg a number of times as Secretary of Labor.[9]

I witnessed another indication that Johnson had used some hyperbole in describing his belief in the importance of the UN. Goldberg had suggested to the President that he invite the Secretary General and the UN diplomatic corps to a White House reception. On Thursday, June 9, 1966, the President called and said he could receive them the following Tuesday! Goldberg told us that, however short the notice and hectic the preparations, we had better make the best of it; the President was not likely to reschedule the reception for any other time. With yeoman efforts on all sides, the UN group arrived at the White House Tuesday evening and were treated to the full splendor of a White House reception. It started with our trip from Andrews Air Force Base to the White House. Our party was preceded by several police cars that cleared the way, ignoring the red lights. We got to the White House in about fifteen minutes.

Unfortunately, halfway through the agonizingly long receiving line—consisting of more than 100 ambassadors and their wives plus a larger number of other dignitaries—the President became bored with the whole exercise and retreated to his private quarters upstairs, until he was persuaded to come back down and finish the job. The Secretary General, who had expected to have a private substantive session with the President, had to settle for a casual chat. By then, of course, Thant's public criticisms of the U.S. actions in Vietnam had not endeared him to either the President or the Secretary of State. Thus, while a visit by the Secretary General and the UN diplomatic corps to the White House was an unprecedented event, it did little to convince the visitors of Johnson's belief in the UN, which, in any case, was not profound.

Still another element in Goldberg's acceptance was the fact that he, the Chicago-born son of a poor Jewish immigrant, would be succeeding the illustrious Adlai Stevenson. In fact, he told some of us at USUN that he would not have considered the job if Stevenson had not been his predecessor.

I suspect, too, that Goldberg, a man of prodigious energy and drive and still in his fifties, did feel a little restless on the court, though I do not doubt his statement that he did not seek the UN job or any other post. Lyndon Johnson wrote in *The Vantage Point* that Goldberg had been "bored" on the Court and wanted to leave.[10] Goldberg became so incensed upon reading this statement that he telephoned the former President and told him in no uncertain terms that Johnson's statement that he had solicited the appointment was completely unfounded, as Johnson had reason to know. He also demanded the return of one of Mrs. Goldberg's paintings that the President had been given after strong hints, stating: "It's mine and you don't deserve it."[11]

In any case, the record shows that Johnson went to great lengths to persuade Goldberg to accept the post, agreed to Goldberg's conditions, and gave him a strong mandate. Moreover, Goldberg had frequent access to the President, long talks with him, and some impact on national policy, at least for the first two years of his tenure. This was particularly true with regard to the Indo-Pakistan War of 1965, the Middle East crisis in 1967, Rhodesia, Southwest Africa, and the *Pueblo* incident (issues discussed later in this chapter). Unfortunately, he had little influence on the main issue that led him to take the UN job—Vietnam.

Goldberg also insisted on having *all* available information on issues confronting the U.S. government. He was keenly aware of Stevenson's acute embarrassment at having to provide false information to the Security Council in the Bay of Pigs incident because he was not privy to the truth and he was determined not to be placed in that position. Also he had been in the OSS during World War II and was thus fully aware of the many sources of intelligence, overt and covert, available to the President. At his insistence, he and his top associates saw not only State Department traffic but also the relevant output of the CIA, the FBI, the Department of Defense, and the National Security Agency. Having the full picture was of enormous importance in developing policy input and in negotiating with other delegations, notably in the Middle East crisis. The National Security Agency intelligence report was brought to me each morning by a naval officer who stood next to my desk while I read it. I then handed the briefing book back to him and he took it to other top officers of the mission.

Overall, I consider Goldberg to have been one of the most effective of the distinguished and capable men who have served as permanent representatives over three decades, during half of which I was at the USUN. As one astute UN correspondent put it, he restored the mission "to a new level of efficiency."[12] He had a creative and retentive mind, prodigious energy, a well-developed sense of organization, and a strong interest in his staff, which had to work extremely hard to keep up with him. His influence with the President—he phoned him often—and Johnson's personal confidence in him meant that Goldberg's well-developed positions on UN issues would often become U.S. policy. Probably about 80 percent of the action proposals and instructions on which USUN operated during his tenure originated with Goldberg or under his guidance. Also, in contrast with the Stevenson era, USUN normally prepared the first draft of speeches, giving it a tactical advantage in bargaining with the State Department in negotiating over the final text.

Goldberg was certainly the best negotiator I have ever seen, at the UN or anywhere else. He was always thoroughly prepared; knowledgeable on all aspects of the issue; aware of what arguments the other side was likely to make; judicious in weighing the strengths and weaknesses of the respective positions; clear in exposition; and calm, patient, and scrupulously honest. This last quality was particularly important at the UN, which is a "glass house" in more ways than one, where bad faith is quickly detected and a reputation for it spreads fast. His long experience with labor negotiations had sharpened his natural talents.

His main weakness was in public speaking, where he compared poorly with Lodge or Stevenson. He had a nasal monotone that sounded dreary in any lengthy public statement, and certain mannerisms made him look pompous. In private discussions and negotiations, however, his keen mind and sensitivity made him a superb interlocutor. Nor should one exaggerate the importance of public speeches at the UN; they rarely change a mind or a vote. The real action is in the private negotiations, especially one-on-one conversations; that is where minds are changed—and that is where Goldberg was at his best.

Goldberg prided himself on good faith negotiations and not "pulling a fast one." For example, on December 19, 1965, a group of African delegations, supported by other anticolonial states and the Soviet bloc, were advancing a resolution calling for the dismantling of all foreign military bases. Their speeches were anticolonial in nature, and privately they told us that the resolution was not aimed at American bases but at colonial bases; however, the text made no such distinction. Consequently, the United States urged that it be amended or withdrawn. We also argued that, if the resolution were put to a vote, a two-thirds majority should be required, since Article 18 of the UN Charter specifies that "recommendations with respect to the maintenance of peace and security" are important questions. The sponsors of the resolution replied, curiously, that the issue was indeed important but not an "important question." Looking around the General Assembly hall I observed that half the African delegations were absent on that Friday afternoon and that we could win the procedural vote. Apparently the Africans present realized the same thing; they asked for a postponement until Monday, December 22. I urged Goldberg to insist on proceeding to a vote, calculating that we could also defeat a motion to adjourn. Also, I had seen the same delegations press relentlessly for a vote when the United States wanted a postponement. But Goldberg, acting as a gentleman, agreed to the postponement. Over the weekend the sponsors lobbied feverishly, using group pressure to enforce anticolonial solidarity and insure the presence of all possible supporters on Monday. As I expected, this made the difference; they won the procedural vote and the resolution was adopted. After its adoption Goldberg made a statement to the Assembly declaring the resolution "ultra vires," since the voting procedures had violated Article 18 of the Charter.

In retrospect I am convinced that Goldberg was right. As a resolution of the General Assembly, the recommendation was not binding on its members, and in fact no state with foreign military bases paid any attention to it. Moreover, even if that resolution had been defeated, a future Assembly would have adopted something similar. By agreeing to the postponement, Goldberg gained a reputation for good sportsmanship and fairness that helped him during the rest of his term at the UN.

Another Goldberg gesture made him popular with Americans in the UN Secretariat. All U.S. permanent representatives had cultivated good relations with the Secretary General, Andrew Cordier, and Ralph Bunche. Also, some of us at USUN developed good working relations with Secretariat officials dealing with our areas of concern. Yet the vast majority of Americans in the Secretariat had little contact with USUN; few had ever been invited there, and many felt neglected or snubbed. Secretariat personnel from most other countries had far more frequent contact with their national missions. I suggested to Goldberg that we do something to improve our relations with Secretariat Americans, and he agreed. In early June 1966 he invited all 1,528 U.S. citizens employed at the UN to an "American Day" reception at the mission and to meet Vice President Humphrey. It was a great success. Few had ever been inside the mission before, and the gesture was appreciated. The guest of honor, Hubert Humphrey, exuded good will and charm. He was just as bouncy, optimistic, and good-humored in private as he was in public. Moreover, Goldberg was able to announce that day the settlement of a grievance by the U.S. employees of the Secretariat, which had previously been brought to his attention by the Secretary General. They had been obliged since 1960 to pay the U.S. social security tax at the high "self-employed" rate, since the UN could not be taxed as an employer. Goldberg, with Humphrey's help, obtained a U.S. government ruling that henceforth they would pay the lower rate charged for employees.[13]

Unfortunately, he was not able to remove one of the handicaps of USUN itself—the sparsity of funds for necessary entertainment. Except for the Russians, there was no other large country on as tight an entertainment budget as the United States. With the fiscal year ending June 30, we had no money for the American Day reception and had to go to private sources.

On other occasions we had to resort to various stratagems. My wife and I would pay off accumulated social obligations by having inexpensive buffets on the top floor of the mission. For two successive years we entertained delegates to the Fourth (Decolonization) Committee by having a wine-tasting party, with free wine and cheese provided by the California Wine Growers Association.

Goldberg wanted to break out of this stodgy pattern of formal dinners and receptions and still live within our tight representation budget. In the fall of 1966, during the General Assembly, he decided to invite foreign delegates to two dinners aboard American passenger ships in port. He asked me to negotiate with the ship company president for "very wholesale" prices. The company was most accommodating, offering a price of $800 for about 200 guests at each party, which would cover the raw cost of the food and beverages used. Unfortunately, at the second dinner a free-loading reporter for a Chicago newspaper started inquiring about the terms offered by a shipping company that received U.S. government subsidies. This disturbed Goldberg, who then instructed me to renegotiate the contract so that we would pay every cent of the full cost. With heavy heart, knowing what a dent it would make in our available funds for the year, I renegotiated for triple the original price!

Goldberg was always sensitive about the press. He read at least four newspapers every day and would react sharply to any adverse story. The veteran newspaperman Frank Carpenter, who served as press officer for Lodge, Stevenson, and Goldberg, advised him not to get excited "just because some guy writes a story in the newspaper," but his advice had little impact on our chief.

THE GOLDBERG TEAM

Initially Goldberg followed the practice of his predecessors, appointing prominent noncareer people at the ambassadorial level, backstopped by experienced professionals. The exception was Career Ambassador Charles Yost, who had been Stevenson's deputy representative to the Security Council and remained in that position under Goldberg. Yost, a superb professional, was Goldberg's principal adviser on political issues, providing a rare incisiveness and sound judgment.

Francis Plimpton, Stevenson's deputy permanent representative and former law school roommate, was as much surprised as any of us when the news of Goldberg's designation came over the news ticker. He apparently expected to stay on and was disappointed when Goldberg accepted his offer to resign. Perhaps in a Freudian slip, he referred to Goldberg a number of times as "Goldwater"; Plimpton was a liberal Republican by conviction and probably had little affection for the leader of the party's right wing.

To replace Plimpton, Goldberg picked Dr. James M. Nabrit, the president of Howard University. Nabrit had been one of the NAACP's top lawyers in the civil rights struggle and was now something of an elder statesman in the black community. While at USUN Nabrit continued as president of Howard and maintained his residence in Washington, commuting back and forth. He did not concern himself much with day-to-day operations, but we all profited from his wisdom.

One factor in Nabrit's appointment was Goldberg's desire to have a distinguished black man in the number two position. Goldberg's appointment came on the heels of outstanding achievements by President Johnson on civil rights, and he was fully in tune with Johnson on this issue. I can recall being at Goldberg's official residence for a Passover seder with diplomats, labor leaders, rabbis, and black leaders where we sang labor songs and "We Shall Overcome." Goldberg also decided we should have a black female on the mission's eleventh (executive) floor and, since my secretary was due to leave, that her replacement should be black. I said the color did not matter as long as she was competent. In due course came Brenda Lee, a beautiful and extremely bright girl, fresh from Saigon. By that time Goldberg had been succeeded by George Ball, who had no interest in Brenda's color, but I did get a bright and good-humored secretary out of the process.

James Roosevelt, eldest son of the late President, became U.S. representative to the UN Economic and Social Council, with the rank of ambassador. A big, outgoing, genial backslapper, a former congressman, Jimmy was very popular with other delegations and a good team man. His one-year tenure corresponded to a period when U.S. economic policy in the UN had become largely defensive and reactive, and this did not fit his activist temperament.

The other ambassadorial slot, representative at the Trusteeship Council, went to Eugenie Anderson, a power in Minnesota politics and an ally of the vice president, Hubert Humphrey. She had previously been ambassador to Bulgaria and Denmark and was skilled in diplomacy as well as politics. During her last year, however, she became heavily involved in Humphrey's 1968 presidential campaign and had little time for her work at the UN. I filled in for her on all colonial issues, although she did return to New York for three weeks in June to serve as President of the Trusteeship Council.

Rounding out the top layer was Richard Pedersen, who had been at USUN since 1953 and had served as chief of the political section. Dick had the rank of minister counselor and continued to concentrate on political issues and the Security Council. I served as deputy counselor, with responsibility for coordinating the missions' activities in the economic, social development, financial, personnel, legal, and decolonization areas. Thus, our office became the nerve center of the mission, as James Barco's office had been under Lodge. Pedersen and I also served as troubleshooters at various UN meetings, either as advisers or as representatives, whenever a situation was important, sensitive, or difficult. (Subsequently Dick became the senior adviser with ambassadorial rank, and I took over as minister counselor.)

Dick Pedersen was a brilliant, intense, hard-working young man. He graduated summa cum laude from the University of the Pacific and got his Ph.D. from Harvard in 1950, at which point he joined the U.S. mission to the UN. He was a stalwart on political and security issues. He later became counselor of the State Department under William Rogers, then Ambassador to Hungary, and eventually President of the American University of Cairo.

Another important member of our team was Admiral John S. McCain, head of our delegation to the Military Staff Committee (MSC) and simultaneously, Commander of the Atlantic Fleet. He had little to do in his nominal job. The MSC, consisting of the Soviet Union, China, Britain, France, and the United States, was envisaged in the UN charter as the body that would oversee enforcement action against an aggressor. It might have had a real role if Germany or Japan had become military aggressors again after World War II. Because of the cold war the five MSC members were never able to agree on the composition and location of forces to be used against an aggressor. Consequently, the MSC met once every two weeks for about half an hour and its only business was to agree to hold the next meeting two weeks later. This ritual was observed because provision for the MSC is in the UN charter. For that task we had a three-star admiral, a Navy captain, one colonel each from the Army and the Air Force, and supporting enlisted personnel. The officers were of high quality, with intelligence backgrounds, and they spent their time collecting intelligence, as did the MSC delegates from the other four countries. One of them, Colonel James Boyd of the Air Force, assisted me in peacekeeping negotiations and later got his Ph.D. from Columbia with a dissertation on UN peacekeeping.

Admiral "Jack" McCain was a brilliant officer who later became CINCPAC (Commander in Chief Pacific, the highest-ranking operational post in the Navy). Physically, he was a small, compact man about five feet five inches tall, but he was a dynamo. During the Six-Day War he provided Goldberg with important immediate information about military operations in the area.

McCain had also acquired a reputation as a highly successful lobbyist for the Navy with Congress. He was known for an impressive lecture on the importance of sea power. Goldberg told him from time to time that he would like to hear that lecture, but the occasion never presented itself until a change-of-command ceremony on an aircraft carrier anchored in New York harbor. There, Goldberg was part of a captive audience and, at long last, heard McCain's speech on sea power.

I was sitting next to another admiral during the ceremony and remarked to him that McCain's service at the UN might be helpful to his career. He laughed and observed, "Are you kidding? When it comes to admirals who know how to drive ships, we can shake them out of the trees. It's his UN exposure and service with Goldberg that makes him a hot property."

McCain's son, also named John S., was a Navy aviator who was shot down over Vietnam and spent many years in a Vietnamese prison. He seems to have survived the experience without any paralyzing bitterness and is now a distinguished senator from Arizona and was a candidate for president.

Also included in our staff were some CIA agents who had cover titles and assignments in the mission. One, Rudolph (Foxy) Carter, served as my deputy in the Economic Committee and made himself quite useful. His prep school friend Frederick (Frecky) Vreeland had a similar function on the political side. They were both men from wealthy families, the types the public often thinks of as typical Foreign Service officers. I had no idea what they did for the CIA, since they had their own channels. A third CIA man, Peter Thacher, did so much work for the mission, particularly with the Outer Space Committee, that the CIA complained. Thereupon he resigned from the CIA and became a regular mission officer. Subsequently he became an official with the UN Environment Program.

Intelligence officers were by no means a monopoly of the United States. All the major powers had them. In fact I used to enjoy conversations with KGB officers from the Soviet mission. They were not afraid of the KGB; hence, they talked more freely.

In 1966 came a major shift. Nabrit had returned to Howard after a year at USUN, and Yost succeeded him as deputy, only to leave shortly thereafter in retirement from the Foreign Service. About the same time, Jimmy Roosevelt resigned to take a job with the Overseas Investor Service in Geneva. Thus the number two, three, and four slots in the mission were open; the expectation of most people, including me, was that they would, as usual, be filled by political appointees. On the contrary, Goldberg decided that he wanted experienced, competent career professionals. As deputy he chose William Buffum, a career Foreign Service officer with many years of experience in the State Department's Bureau of International Organization Affairs. Buffum had been deputy to Joseph Sisco, then assistant secretary for International Organization Affairs, who recommended him. Dick Pedersen became deputy representative to the UN Security Council.

Goldberg offered me the post of representative to the UN Economic and Social Council (ECOSOC) vacated by Roosevelt. The offer was tempting, since I had found dealing with economic issues at the UN highly gratifying; however, family considerations would have made it difficult to spend long periods abroad at meetings of ECOSOC and its various subsidiary and affiliate bodies. I therefore suggested to Goldberg that he offer the ECOSOC slot to Eugenie Anderson. If she wanted it, I would take her place as representative to the Trusteeship Council, while continuing as executive coordinator of the mission and of the General Assembly delegations, as well as general troubleshooter. He agreed to ask her, and she took several weeks to think about it. In the meantime, President Johnson decided to offer the ECOSOC job to an old friend, Arthur ("Tex") Goldschmidt, who had spent many years in the UN Secretariat dealing with economic and technical assistance matters. Thus, Eugenie was foreclosed from shifting and remained for a time as representative to the Trusteeship Council. Goldberg decided that he would nevertheless nominate me for ambassadorial rank as senior adviser, in which capacity I did in fact deal with many issues of decolonization and trusteeship, as well as political, economic, peacekeeping, legal, budget, and personnel questions.

The new team of predominantly career ambassadors was sworn in on January 27, 1967, marking a new departure for U.S. representation initiated by Goldberg. As a team it was the hardest-working and most competent group of top assistants I saw during fifteen years at the mission—a judgment I could make leaving myself out of the calculation. Our standard working day was about twelve hours; Goldberg worked longer. This strength was to prove particularly important during the Middle East crisis, including the Six-Day War in June 1967, which we shall discuss later in this chapter.

Another feature of the Goldberg era at USUN was the mobilization of the wives. President Johnson depended significantly on his wife and set a style in Washington for wives of the cabinet officers to help their husbands in their jobs—a style that Goldberg characterized as "two for the price of one." Dorothy Goldberg plunged energetically and wholeheartedly into her part of the job, not only at social functions hosted jointly by her husband, but also at coffees and teas for the wives of foreign diplomats at the Goldbergs' official residence in the Waldorf Tower and in visits to foreign wives who had suffered family calamities or tragedies. She also enlisted the services of our wives, some of whom had other responsibilities that made the added social duties a hardship. In her book Mrs. Goldberg writes that she "related better to foreign wives than to our own."[14] One reason was that some of "our own" had to live in the suburbs because we had neither rent allowances nor government-paid quarters. Arriving at midtown at 10:00 A.M., well groomed and well coifed for a morning coffee session with foreign wives, after a late official dinner the night before, was not a joyous event, particularly since the wife usually had no servants and had to keep her own household running. Yet, like her husband, Dorothy Goldberg worked hardest of any of the wives, and I can remember fondly her bringing us sandwiches and coffee during a midnight break at the Security Council.

Another Goldberg innovation was a monthly report to the two living former presidents, Truman and Eisenhower. These reports, known by the staff as the "Harry and Ike letters," kept the two men regularly informed of all significant developments and invited their comments. Truman, by then very advanced in years, sent polite acknowledgments but no substantive comments. Eisenhower, on the other hand, frequently gave views and opinions in his letters of reply. In any case, it was a wise stroke on Goldberg's part, helping to build bipartisan sympathies for American policies at the UN.

ARTICLE 19

It was left for Goldberg finally to break the Article 19 deadlock discussed in the previous chapter. By the time he came on the scene in July 1965, it was obvious that there was no way the General Assembly would apply the loss-of-vote sanction in Article 19 of the Charter to those countries that were two years in arrears in paying their assessments because they would not pay their share of the Middle East and Congo peacekeeping operations.

Goldberg shuttled back and forth between New York and Washington to take soundings with key congressmen, the State Department, the secretary general, other delegations, and his own staff. All were agreed that the General Assembly must assume its normal activity in September, including voting. Goldberg's preference, which eventually prevailed, was to make a statement in August to the Special Committee on Peacekeeping Operations outlining the legal correctness of the U.S. position but indicating that in view of the apparent consensus of the General Assembly not to bring the

Article 19 question to a decision, the United States would not seek to frustrate the consensus. There was a general agreement with this position at USUN, although some of us also felt that there would be no great tragedy in raising the issue as a matter of principle and losing, if this would sit better with Congress. Goldberg, however, was concerned that there might be a strong reaction in Congress and among the American people against the UN if the United States were defeated on such an issue. He succeeded in persuading the key congressmen to go along. He also journeyed to Gettysburg and persuaded Eisenhower, who was preparing to attack the proposed course of action, not to do so and to help in meeting congressional reaction.[15]

Accordingly, Goldberg made his statement ending the impasse on August 16, 1965 to the Special Committee on Peacekeeping Operations. After reviewing the history of the General Assembly's actions in assessing the costs, the advisory opinion of the International Court of Justice (ICJ) supporting the Assembly's actions, the Assembly's vote by an overwhelming majority to accept the ICJ's opinion, and its evident unwillingness to apply Article 19, Goldberg declared:

The United States regretfully concludes, on ample evidence, that at this stage in the history of the United Nations the General Assembly is not prepared to carry out the relevant provisions of the Charter in the context of the present situation. From private consultations, from statements by the principal officers of the Organization, from the statements and exhaustive negotiations within and outside this Committee, from an informal polling of the delegations—indeed from the entire history of this affair—the inevitable conclusion is that the Assembly is not disposed to apply the loss-of-vote sanction of Article 19 to the present situation.

We regret exceedingly that the intransigence of a few of the Member States, and their unwillingness to abide by the rule of law, has led the Organization into this state of affairs.

The United States adheres to the position that Article 19 is applicable in the present circumstances. It is clear, however, that we are faced with a simple and inescapable fact of life which I have just cited. Moreover, every parliamentary body must decide, in one way or another, the issues that come before it; otherwise it will have no useful existence, and soon no life.

Therefore, without prejudice to the position that Article 19 is applicable, the United States recognizes, as it simply must, that the General Assembly is not prepared to apply Article 19 in the present situation and that the consensus of the membership is that the Assembly should proceed normally. We will not seek to frustrate that consensus, since it is not in the world interest to have the work of the General Assembly immobilized in these troubled days. At the same time, we must make it crystal clear that if any member can insist on making an exception to the principle of collective financial responsibility with respect to certain activities of the Organization, the United States reserves the same option to make exceptions if, in our view, strong and compelling reasons exist for doing so. There can be no double standard among the members of the Organization.[16]

Until recent years the United States did not exercise this option. Now, however, the United States owes over a billion dollars in unpaid dues and this shortfall has had a devastating effect on the UN's ability to pay for its operations. I believed then, and even more strongly now, that we should have defended Article 19 then to the end, win or lose. Thus, the authority of the General Assembly on financial matters has been weakened, especially with regard to the major powers.

THE INDO-PAKISTAN WAR—1965

The outbreak in August 1965 of large-scale hostilities between India and Pakistan quickly demonstrated the need for a fully functioning UN. Because the presidency rotates monthly in alphabetical order, Goldberg happened to be president of the Security Council when the question came there in September. Drawing on his experience in settling labor disputes, he emphasized the importance of private negotiations among the members to reach agreement rather than making speeches at each other in the Council chamber. The result was a cease-fire agreement that a new group of UN observers had some difficulty in persuading the parties to carry out.[17]

Ruth Russell gives the following succinct summary of ensuing events:

At that time, both Soviet Union and the United States wanted to keep the violence from spreading; but Communist China supported Pakistan's truculence and accused Moscow of conspiring with Washington to dominate the world through the United Nations. The withholding of foreign economic and military aid from both parties succeeded in forcing an end to the fighting before a military decision. (Although India appears to have been leading at the time, both sides later claimed to be winning.) Perhaps to avoid the Chinese charges, the Soviet Union offered its good offices to the two governments in direct negotiations. President Ayub and Premier Shastri accepted, meeting in Tashkent in November 1965 with Premier Kosygin. This effort resulted in a formal accord, most importantly to withdraw to military positions held prior to the outbreak of hostilities; but politically little was accomplished except to open a door through which further negotiations might be undertaken. Unfortunately, the sudden death of the Indian Prime Minister, immediately after signature of the agreement, made further progress more difficult. Certain measures to restore economic relations were about all the advance made.[18]

RHODESIA

Goldberg had an important impact on American policy toward Rhodesia. He helped in moving Washington to strong support of majority rule and against the Ian Smith white minority regime.

In October 1965, perceiving signs of an early unilateral declaration of independence by Smith, a group of new nations rushed through the General

Assembly a resolution condemning any attempt by the Rhodesians to seize independence and calling upon the United Kingdom to use all possible means to prevent such a declaration.[19] The United States voted in favor, along with the overwhelming majority; only Portugal and South Africa voted against the resolution; France abstained and the United Kingdom did not participate in the voting. When the white Rhodesians went ahead anyway, the Assembly adopted a resolution that condemned "the unilateral declaration of independence made by the racialist minority in Southern Rhodesia" and recommended that the Security Council consider the situation as a matter of urgency.[20] At the request of the United Kingdom the Security Council met on November 12, 1965 to consider the Rhodesian situation. Thus, the British were finally abandoning their position that neither the United Kingdom nor the United Nations had the right to interfere in the territory's internal affairs. During November 1965 the Security Council passed resolutions that condemned the unilateral declaration of independence, called upon all states to refrain from recognizing or assisting the regime, requested all states to break economic relations with Southern Rhodesia, and requested the establishment of an embargo on oil and petroleum products to Southern Rhodesia.[21]

The resolution on the oil embargo was a compromise between a British draft and one submitted by 36 African states. The African draft called for the *mandatory* employment of "all enforcement measures" and a finding that the situation in Rhodesia constituted a threat to international peace. This was the language of UN Charter Chapter VII and implied that the use of force could be among the measures contemplated—much further than the British were willing to go. Goldberg suggested rephrasing the statement to read that "the situation . . . is of extreme seriousness . . . its continuance in time constitutes a threat to peace and security." This was the language of Chapter VI, which envisages seeking solutions by negotiations and other means of peaceful settlement. Also, members were *requested* to apply the embargo, not ordered to do so at that stage. (Later, mandatory sanctions were ordered by the Council.) The Africans agreed to accept Goldberg's language both because it avoided a British veto and because it could be interpreted to mean that, if the situation persisted, the Security Council could reopen discussion of the question of mandatory and more pervasive sanctions or even force. This was a typical example of Goldberg's skill as a negotiator, using careful ambiguity, his acceptability on both sides, and his policy clout in Washington.

During the following year the United Kingdom negotiated with Smith on the principle of No Independence before Majority Rule (NIBMAR), but the negotiations failed. Under strong African pressure the United Kingdom in December 1966 asked the Security Council to approve for the first time since its founding selective, mandatory sanctions against a regime. During a week of discussion the African states made a concerted attempt to alter the British draft drastically to include more commodities and to provide enforcement provisions in insure that the Council's edict was carried out. The African states also sought to have the Security Council deplore the British refusal to use force against Rhodesia and to call upon the United Kingdom to withdraw all previous offers to the Rhodesian regime and to declare flatly that it would grant independence to Rhodesia only under majority rule.

Although the British successfully resisted the African attempt to have the Security Council order the use of force and dictate the terms of settlement, the Africans did succeed through amendments in strengthening economic sanctions in the resolution. On December 16, by a vote of 11 to 0, with Bulgaria, France, Mali, and the Soviet Union abstaining, the Security Council approved a ban on the purchase of twelve of Rhodesia's chief exports and the supply to Rhodesia of oil and oil products. Not only did this mark the first use of mandatory sanctions by the Security Council, but the Council itself emerged as a new instrument in the politics of decolonization.

Goldberg sincerely believed in the sanctions approach. In our strategy meetings at USUN and his policy discussions with Washington, he drew a parallel with the American South, where economic pressures had helped significantly in the civil rights struggle. He also argued that U.S. trade and investment in black Africa and Rhodesia would become increasingly important; consequently, on both moral and practical grounds, the United States should support the economic sanctions. Goldberg knew, too, that Britain would not use force against the Smith regime, as demanded by the Africans, and he considered it important, therefore, to support the economic sanctions that the British offered as an alternative means toward majority rule. The British, who were not likely to have used armed forces anyway, were warned by Undersecretary of State George Ball that the United States would not bail them out if a "quick-kill" action hurt their balance of payments.

Goldberg had to wage a strong policy battle in Washington on the sanctions issues. Aligned against him were Defense; NASA (concerned about its tracking stations in South Africa); Commerce; and Treasury, the latter two because of economic considerations. This time, however, the State Department had a solid front in supporting sanctions, despite the misgivings of Undersecretary George Ball. The assistant secretary of state for African affairs, Mennen Williams, and his deputy, Wayne Fredericks, were strong and determined, and they found strong allies in International Organization Affairs (IO) and Legal (L), as well as the staff of the National Security Council. This time European Affairs (EUR) went along willingly, since the British wanted the sanctions. In this battle within the Washington bureaucracy, Goldberg's interventions were highly important especially after Williams and Ball left in 1966. Then it was Goldberg who provided leadership to the prosanctions groups, ably backstopped in Washington by Joseph

Sisco, the IO assistant secretary, who was both vigorously assertive and completely responsive to Goldberg's lead.[22]

Goldberg had to answer many American critics, notably Dean Acheson, who considered the sanctions a dangerous precedent for similar action whenever violations of human rights were involved. Goldberg argued that there were a number of unique elements in the Rhodesian situation.

Here we have witnessed an illegal seizure of power by a small minority bent on perpetuating the subjugation of the vast majority. Moreover, in this situation the sovereign authority with international responsibility for the territory has asked the United Nations to take measures which will permit the restoration of the full rights of the people of this territory under the Charter. . . .

Law in the United Nations, as in our own society, is often developed on a case-by-case basis. We should analyze each action of the UN political organs with due regard for the facts of each case and be careful of hasty generalizations. Because the Security Council considers the situation in Rhodesia, with its unique legal and factual elements, as constituting a threat to the peace requiring the application of mandatory sanctions, does not absolve it from an independent exercise of judgment in different situations.

Moreover, each of the Permanent Members of the Security Council has the power to prevent the use of enforcement measures in other situations where it may deem them to be inappropriate.[23]

The Security Council subsequently established a committee of all fifteen members to monitor compliance with the sanctions, report violations, and make recommendations to the council.[24] It also added to the economic sanctions until they became virtually total. In the initial years the United States, along with the United Kingdom, supported the committee's activities wholeheartedly, not only with implementing action of its own, but also with reports, including information from intelligence sources, about violations by others. This caused some irritation to Japan and certain European countries, mostly western and some eastern, where forbidden Rhodesian goods were entering in substantial quantities. Nevertheless, throughout Goldberg's term the United States continued its energetic support for the sanctions. I was U.S. member of the committee until August 1971 and served as its chairman for a time.

The sanctions did not budge the Smith regime in Rhodesia. Portugal denounced them as contrary to the UN Charter, since the resolution mandating the sanctions did not have "the concurrence of the permanent members," as called for in Article 27, paragraph 3. France and the Soviet Union had abstained. If the language of that article is read literally, the Portuguese interpretations would be correct; however, the practice at the UN for 20 years had been to consider a Security Council resolution validly adopted if it had the required majority and no permanent member voted against it. (It will be recalled that the Soviets were boycotting the Security Council in

June 1950 when the Council approved a resolution calling on member states to provide troops, supplies, or services to help repulse the North Korean invasion.) Consequently, the Portuguese argument was rejected by the secretary general, obviously supported by practice and by the membership in general. Indeed, the practice of not considering abstention or nonvoting by a permanent member as a veto has continued to this day; changing it would seriously hobble the effectiveness of the Security Council.

Nevertheless, Portugal refused to comply with the sanctions, and the ports of its "province" of Mozambique were used fully by neighboring Rhodesia. South Africa also provided Rhodesia with transit and port facilities, as it helped generally to sustain the illegal Smith regime. Rhodesian products, especially chrome, the principal export, were transshipped from South Africa under fraudulent certificates of origin describing them as South African products. Importers did not examine the documents too closely, as the terms were generally advantageous to them, nor did the officials of most importing countries. Moreover, vehicles and other goods needed by Rhodesia were obtained through South Africa and Mozambique, often at higher prices because of the need for transshipment and fraudulent documents. Many products formerly imported began to be manufactured in Rhodesia, usually at a higher price than had been paid for imports before sanctions were imposed. Thus, Rhodesia suffered some economic inconvenience from the sanctions, but the pressure did not bring the Smith regime to submit or to change its racist policy.[25] The Africans in the committee and on the Security Council, therefore, demanded the extension of sanctions to Portugal and South Africa and British use of force to bring Smith down. The British, backed by the United States and other Western allies, refused these demands. Their zeal for the existing sanctions against Smith was at least in part an effort to placate the Africans without taking the steps demanded.

Throughout Johnson's term the United States supported the British policy of sanctions and stayed one step behind them. This policy and Goldberg's relations with the Africans were remarkably successful. Majority rule was achieved in Rhodesia (now Zimbabwe) without the use of force.

THE SIX-DAY WAR

Goldberg's role in negotiating with Soviet Foreign Minister Gromyko and Ambassador Dobrynin during the 1967 Middle East crisis has been called "the apogee of his career at the UN."[26] In fact, his role throughout the crisis could be described as his finest hour at the UN.

In May 1967 the Soviet Union warned Egyptian authorities that Israel was preparing to attack Syria. Reports by UN truce observers (UNTSO) failed to find any evidence of such preparations, and the Soviet ambassador to Israel refused an Israeli invitation to visit the Syrian border to see for himself. Meanwhile, President Nasser was being taunted by other Arab leaders for hiding behind the protection of the UN Emergency Force (UNEF) in the Sinai. Nasser used the unconfirmed (and probably untrue) Soviet report as a reason for placing Egyptian forces in a state of readiness and, on May 18, demanding the withdrawal of UNEF; both actions were contrary to the 1956–1957 armistice agreements.[27] It is noteworthy that neither Syria nor the Soviet Union saw fit to bring the alleged Israeli threat to the attention of the Security Council. Israel, under threat of strangulation, saw one outside guarantee after another vanish. She had withdrawn her forces from the Sinai in 1957 on two understandings: (1) that a UN force would keep her border with Egypt tranquil and the Gulf of Aqaba open; (2) that the major maritime powers would guarantee access to Aqaba.

On June 1, Secretary General U Thant acceded promptly to Nasser's request for withdrawal of the force, an action subsequently attacked sharply by critics and defended staunchly by U Thant.

There is no doubt whatsoever that U Thant had to withdraw the force if Nasser was sufficiently determined to oust it. A lightly armed force of 5,000 men, sent to keep peace, not to fight, and dependent for logistics on the Egyptians—such a force could not have resisted a determined Egyptian army. If the two sides were determined to fight, leaving UNEF would only have exposed its troops to fruitless casualties and might have done permanent damage to the willingness of states to provide contingents for any future UN peacekeeping operations.

Moreover, the contingents of India and Yugoslavia—countries tightly aligned with Egypt as leaders of the nonaligned—had already pulled out of the line without waiting for the secretary general to act, leaving only about half the force there.

The only real question, therefore, is whether Thant had to respond so promptly. I felt at the time—and still do—that he should have played for more time. President Nasser, three years after the Six-Day War, told a correspondent that he did not want the whole force withdrawn, only part of it.[28] Whether or not this statement is taken at face value, Thant might have volunteered to go to Cairo to discuss the matter, perhaps giving Nasser a face-saving way of backing down. This is speculation, of course, but it is hard to see why even this slight possibility was left unexplored.[29]

So the force was withdrawn, and the first understanding, dating back to 1956–1957, vanished.

On June 2, the United States consulted the other Western maritime powers about action to fulfill the pledge that Aqaba would be kept open to all shipping. I saw the replies. One government after another found reasons not to act. It was said around the U.S. mission to the UN, not entirely in jest, that the fleet of maritime powers that could be assembled would consist of a Dutch admiral commanding an American destroyer (our navy was heavily committed to Vietnam and elsewhere). London and Washington did issue statements on behalf of the maritime powers protesting the announced blockade of Aqaba, but these were peremptorily rejected by Egypt.[30]

U Thant learned of the blockade while en route to Cairo on May 22, *following* his decision to terminate UNEF. Upon his return to New York he alerted the Council to the fact that Israel considered the blockade a *casus belli*. He then stated:

In my view, a peaceful outcome to the present crisis will depend upon a breathing spell which will allow tension to subside from its present explosive level. I therefore urge all the parties concerned to exercise special restraint, to forgo belligerence and to avoid all other actions which could increase tension, to allow the Council to deal with the underlying causes of the present crisis and to seek solutions.[31]

The United States, along with Argentina, Brazil, Canada, Denmark, and the United Kingdom, consulted other Council members on a draft resolution calling on all parties "to forgo belligerence" (i.e., not blockade Aqaba) in order to provide a "breathing spell" that would "allow the Council to deal with the underlying causes of the present crisis and to seek solutions." This proposal had the support of at least nine of the fifteen members—the required majority unless a permanent member casts a veto. In the Council when Ambassador Goldberg pleaded for such action without delay, the Soviet representative (Fedorenko), echoed by Bulgaria, accused him of creating "hysteria" and argued that there was no cause for excitement. India, apparently reflecting Nasser's views, also denied any urgency. Thus, the Council was stymied right up to the very eve of the outbreak of fighting—another fact that Israel remembered.

Though the Council was stymied, this was a time of feverish activity at USUN. In fact, from May 15, when Nasser requested UNEF's withdrawal, to August 15, I had one Saturday and one Sunday off, on different weekends, and we had numerous Council sessions that went into the next morning. Goldberg was a stickler for advance planning, complete information, meticulous preparation, and full consultation with other delegations.

One vivid recollection stands out. On Sunday, June 4, we had just been to an afternoon meeting of cooperative delegations at the Danish mission on Third Avenue and Forty-second Street and had managed to arrive at a "breathing spell" draft resolution that could command the necessary nine-vote majority. As we walked up Second Avenue on our way back to USUN, someone had a pocket radio with the news turned on. It was reported that the Israeli troops were relaxing at the beaches. Goldberg commented: "I don't like that. With the Israeli mobilization system they could be ready in two hours." How prophetic!

Meanwhile, President Johnson had been very active in trying to prevent the war. To the end of his term, he made it clear to Israeli officials that he regretted their decision to go to war on June 5. On May 22, 1967, when Nasser announced the blockade, he sent Prime Minister Kosygin a strong message urging a maximum effort in the cause of moderation. He underlined the danger that American and Soviet ties to nations in the Middle East could bring about difficulties neither wanted, not only in the Middle East but elsewhere. During the war itself, American forces in the Mediterranean were strengthened and directed to within 50 miles of the Syrian coast when a June 10 message from Moscow raised the possibility of Soviet military intervention. But the major business between Moscow and Washington over the hot line was, in effect, a high-level review of what was going on in New York, that is, an attempt to achieve a cease-fire.[32]

In an effort to prevent war, Johnson sent former Ambassador Charles Yost to Cairo in late May. Yost reported that the Egyptian leaders were dismayed by what they had themselves wrought. They were aware that the Aqaba blockade might be treated as a *casus belli* by Israel. They were by no means ready for war, yet hesitated to lose face in the Arab world. Consequently, they welcomed the suggestion of an exchange of vice presidential visits with the United States, and the Egyptian vice president was preparing to go to Washington as the first step in the exchange. Yost believed they were looking for a face-saving way out of the crisis they had precipitated, with Soviet encouragement. But war broke out before the visit could take place.

When fighting broke out on June 5, the U.S. delegation moved promptly that morning to get Council agreement on a resolution calling, as a first step, for an immediate cease-fire. Once again there was opposition from the USSR, Bulgaria, and India, which insisted that the resolution also call for withdrawal to the June 4 positions. The entire day and evening were spent in wrangling and negotiations, while both the Israelis and the Egyptians told Council members around the fringes of the chamber that their armies were having great success. The most intensive negotiations took place between the United States and the USSR, the latter apparently carrying the proxy of the UAR; these were adjourned overnight, at Fedorenko's request.

Because we were getting full and accurate information about the fighting, we had no difficulty in agreeing to Fedorenko's request for delay. Just before going into the room for negotiations with the Soviets that evening, I had asked Ambassador Joel Barromi of the Israeli delegation how things were going. He had just phoned Jerusalem and said: "We are picking up more shoes than we did in 1956." (The retreating Egyptian soldiers discarded their shoes so they could run faster.) This corresponded to the reports from the U.S. sources. I advised Goldberg to stand firm on our draft resolution text, and this was his own inclination as well. When Federenko asked for adjournment, Goldberg and I exchanged knowing glances of satisfaction.

By the next morning, June 6, the rout of the Egyptian forces was evident. We had also received an intercept of a Moscow instruction to Fedorenko to accept the U.S. draft. When Fedorenko phoned Goldberg to signify his acceptance, Goldberg—the shrewd and careful negotiator—said, "Fine, Nikolai, now we must agree on the interpretation." Thus, the initial U.S. draft, calling for a cease-fire in place, was accepted by the Soviets and adopted by the Council on June 6.

It is interesting to conjecture what might have happened if this resolution had been adopted on the morning of June 5 when it was originally proposed and Israel had not advanced very far into the Sinai. Later that week similar cease-fire resolutions called for a halt to fighting between Israel and Jordan and Syria, respectively. Much credit was due to Hans Tabor, of Denmark, who presided with great skill over the Council's deliberations in the month of June. It was he who presented the laboriously negotiated cease-fire resolutions as presidential proposals, thus facilitating unanimous adoption.

The Soviet delegation, while accepting the cease-fire resolutions adopted by the Council for the three fighting fronts, continually pressed for the condemnation of Israel as the "aggressor" and for the immediate withdrawal of all forces to the lines existing on June 4. Goldberg and others on the Council resisted such a one-sided condemnation, noting that the blockade of Aqaba and other Egyptian actions could hardly make that country an innocent party. Withdrawal to the June 4 lines would only restore the dangerous situation of that date. Goldberg also argued that the Council must go beyond the immediate crisis and seek a stable peace. This position was supported not only by Canada, Denmark, and Britain but also by Argentina, Brazil, China, Ethiopia, and Nigeria, in part as a result of intensive consultations and Goldberg's skill and persuasiveness.

Goldberg again showed his mettle on June 10. The Council met at 4:30 A.M. on a Syrian complaint that Israel was violating the June 10 cease-fire, advancing farther into Syria, and bombing Damascus. Fedorenko, the Soviet representative, demanded immediate condemnation of Israel and introduced a draft resolution to that effect. Goldberg argued that the Council needed authentic information and urged that General Bull, the UNTSO commander, be asked to report. Even after Bull reported that an air attack against Damascus was going on, Goldberg remained calm. He raised questions as to whether the report was based on firsthand information and whether reported Syrian artillery fire on Israeli villages had been verified (U.S. intelligence had indicated the latter). What was needed, he said, was a comprehensive report as to what was going on in the entire area. Further reports from Bull indicated that there had been some bombing seven to ten kilometers south of Damascus, about fifteen minutes after the agreed cease-fire, and that an hour and a half after the agreed cease-fire time there was continued artillery fire from Syria on positions in Israel. Bull also reported that the Israeli defense minister, Dayan, told him that Israel would implement any cease-fire proposals made by Bull. The Soviets introduced a resolution condemning Israel. Goldberg, pointing to the violations by both sides, won support for revising the Soviet text. As a result, resolution 236 (1967), as adopted unanimously on June 12, condemned "any and all violations of the cease-fire" (Goldberg's language). It also reaffirmed the cease-fire and called for the prompt return of troops to their positions of June 10 and full cooperation with the UN Truce Supervision Organization in implementing the cease-fire. This time the truce held.

On June 14 the Soviets introduced a draft resolution, which "vigorously" condemned Israel's "aggression" and demanded that Israel "should immediately and unconditionally remove all its troops . . . and withdraw them behind the armistice lines."[33] Goldberg argued that it would be unrealistic to expect Israel to act as if there were peace, by withdrawing its troops, while the Arab states continued to insist that there was a state of belligerency—Nasser's justification for blockading Aqaba. This line of reasoning had majority support. When the Soviet draft was put to the vote on June 14, it was supported by only four states—Bulgaria, India, Mali, and the Soviet Union itself—with nine votes required for adoption.[34]

Fedorenko thereupon announced that, the Council having failed, the Soviets would request an emergency special session of the General Assembly. He insisted on this course even though other draft resolutions were still before the Council, including a U.S. draft that, Goldberg stated, was open for discussion, modification, and revision. Ironically, the only relevant rule of procedure for convening an emergency session had been inserted under the Uniting for Peace resolution of 1950, a resolution the Soviet Union had so often denounced because it was related to the UN action in Korea and because Moscow maintains, as a matter of principle, that only the Security Council may take action to deal with the maintenance of peace or threats to international peace and security.

One hour before the Assembly began its first substantive session on June 19, 1967, President Johnson made a speech over all media laying down the fundamental policy of the United States. He declared that peace in the Middle East must be made by the parties themselves and that it must be based on five principles:

- first, the recognized right of national life;
- second, justice for the refugees;
- third, innocent maritime passage;
- fourth, limits on the wasteful and destructive arms race;
- and fifth, political independence and territorial integrity for all.

American policy since that date has been based on those principles as well as on the concept that peace must be made by the parties themselves.

Variations have occurred mainly on the question of how much outside assistance, mediation, or prodding might be helpful.

Debate at the 1967 emergency session centered largely on two draft resolutions—one, sponsored by Yugoslavia, India, and a group of "nonaligned" countries, was close to the United Arab Republic (UAR) desiderata, that is, immediate, unconditional withdrawal of all Israeli forces to June 4 positions; the second, sponsored by a group of Latin American countries, linked withdrawal by Israel of "all its forces from the territories occupied by it as a result of the recent conflict" to ending "the state of belligerency."[35] The vote on the first was 53 in favor, 46 against, and 20 abstentions; on the second, 57 in favor, 43 against, and 20 abstentions. Since this was an important question requiring a two-thirds majority, neither was adopted. The superficial observer might conclude that the session was thus a failure. In my view, it was a highly significant exercise, more so than at other sessions when resolutions were adopted that obviously could have no effect. The result was a general recognition that if Israel were to act as if there were a state of peace by withdrawing from good defensive positions, the Arab states concerned could not persist in a state of belligerency vis-à-vis Israel. Thus, the groundwork was laid for Security Council resolution 242 of November 22, 1967—the only basis for solution accepted unanimously by the Council and by the nations directly concerned.

Another significant result of the emergency session was the decisive rejection of Soviet and Albanian resolutions that sought to brand Israel as an aggressor.

In the latter stages of the emergency session the Soviets initiated bilateral negotiations with the United States in an endeavor to find a generally acceptable formula. The Soviets chose their ambassador to Washington, Anatoly Dobrynin, to lead their side, apparently because they had more confidence in him that in Nikolai Fedorenko, their ambassador to the UN. But when Dobrynin suggested negotiations with Secretary of State Dean Rusk, he was advised that Ambassador Goldberg had the responsibility for the United States. The Dobrynin-Goldberg negotiations proceeded very well in New York; a draft resolution was worked out that was acceptable to the UAR, Jordan, the Soviet Union, and the United States—but not to Israel. The United States was nevertheless ready to go forward with it; however, violent opposition from Algeria and Iraq caused the UAR to draw back. The Soviets—with evident reluctance and discomfort—abandoned the endeavor, much to the relief of Israel.

Yet these negotiations were not in vain. Along with the Latin American resolution, referred to above, they helped to pave the way for the Security Council action in November.

During the general debate of the twenty-second general session of the General Assembly, progress was made toward understanding among the prime ministers and foreign ministers of the interested countries. Consequently, when the Security Council met in November to consider the Middle East question, it was able to build upon the Latin American resolution of the emergency session; the Soviet, American, UAR, and Jordan discussions of July; and the discreet private sessions that took place during the general debate.

The resolution finally agreed upon unanimously in the Security Council was put forward by Lord Caradon, the British representative, but the draft was largely Goldberg's.[36] Virtually all fifteen members of the Council engaged in the consultations that resulted in the agreed text, with critical negotiations taking place between Goldberg, Lord Caradon, and Vasily Kuznetzov, the Soviet first deputy foreign minister.

Since the various parties have given different interpretations of the text, it might be well at this point to refer to the Security Council records of the discussion that took place there. Most of the controversy about resolution 242 has revolved around paragraph 1 concerning "withdrawal of Israeli armed forces from territories occupied in the recent conflict." The Arabs and Soviets have claimed that this means *all* territories. I know from my own experience with the negotiations that the resolution would not have been accepted by a substantial number of members of the Security Council and certainly not by Israel if the word "all" had appeared. This is what Lord Caradon alluded to when he introduced the draft resolution to the Security Council on November 20 and said, "Since then I have been strongly pressed by both sides—I emphasize, by both sides—to make changes particularly in the provisions regarding withdrawal. But I came to the conclusion that to make variations under pressure from one side or the other at this stage would destroy the equal balance which we had endeavored to achieve and would also destroy the confidence which we hope to build on our effort to be just and impartial."[37]

These beneficial results of a General Assembly session that started on an ominous note for Israel were not an accident. Goldberg and his team worked prodigiously to turn around a substantial number of delegations that initially were prepared to support the India-Yugoslavia resolution, enough to deny the two-thirds majority required. This took literally hundreds of one-on-one contacts. During that assembly we worked seven days a week, twelve hours a day to get the job done. Even the Latin American resolution, which drew votes away from the India Yugoslavia draft, was a result of consultations between Goldberg and Pat Solomon of Trinidad, who became the able leader of the Latin Americans on this issue. I still feel proud of the job we did under Goldberg's leadership.

When it became clear that the Soviets would not achieve their objective at the Emergency Session, they wanted to close it down as soon as possible. But they ran into objections from some Arab states, and that delayed closure. I recall with some amusement an incident when a Soviet representative complained to me: "How can you deal with these Arabs?" This seemed ironic considering the consistent Soviet support of the Arabs. Another thing that became clear during that Emergency Session was that none of the Arab states really cared about the Palestinians. They were concerned only about their own interests. The UN is as much a political arena as is the world that surrounds it.

It is ironic that the Latin American resolution, which failed to get the required two-thirds majority at the fifth emergency special session of the General Assembly in July because it was strongly opposed by the Arabs and their friends, was actually more favorable to the Arab position than resolution 242. The former called for the withdrawal of forces from *all* occupied territories. Even the text agreed to by Goldberg and Dobrynin on July 19 called upon "all parties to the conflict to withdraw without delay their forces from *the* territories occupied by them after June 4, 1967" (italics mine).[38]

There is some irony in the fact that Goldberg, a Zionist sympathizer, had the principal role in negotiating the cease-fire resolutions and the basis for a settlement, resolution 242. Many American Jews regretted that he was placed in that role, fearing that Goldberg would lean over backward to prove that he was objective. In fact, his fairness was recognized by the Arabs; only Ambassador Tomeh of Syria attacked him personally in the Security Council debates, and Syria was so virulently anti-American at that time that its representative would have attacked any U.S. representative. By contrast, the Egyptian representative, Ambassador El Kony, was personally very friendly with Goldberg. The two would usually embrace when they met in the corridor after bitter Security Council debates on the Middle East in 1967.

It is also significant that President Johnson and Secretary of State Rusk consciously gave Goldberg the main responsibility for the Middle East negotiations. As noted above, the Soviets, who had more confidence in the negotiating ability of their ambassador to Washington (Dobrynin) than their UN representative (Fedorenko), were directed to Goldberg when they sought bilateral talks, and Dobrynin came to New York for talks with Goldberg. One factor may have been that Johnson and Rusk were deeply involved with the war in Vietnam, then at its peak, while Goldberg could concentrate on the Middle East. Even so, Johnson's delegation of authority to Goldberg was a mark of great confidence, which, from my own observation, was well placed.

THE UN INTERNATIONAL CONVENTION AGAINST RACIAL DISCRIMINATION

In December 1965, the United States was faced with a difficult situation. A resolution was introduced in the Third Committee that incorporated a draft International Convention on the Elimination of All Forms of Racial

Discrimination. Article 4 (b) contained a provision that states parties shall "declare illegal and prohibit organizations and also organized and all other propaganda activities which promote and incite racial discrimination and shall recognize participation in such organizations or activities as an offense punishable by law." This provision runs counter to the First Amendment of the U.S. Constitution and we could not accept it. Yet it would look bad if the U.S. voted against a convention against racial discrimination.

Our representative on this issue was William Rogers, Attorney General in the Eisenhower administration and later Secretary of State under Nixon. Bill and I concocted two amendments, one that would eliminate Article 4 (b) and which he put forth as a U.S. amendment. The other added to 4 (b) the phrase "with due regard to the principles embodied in the Universal Declaration of Human Rights and the rights expressly set forth in Article 5 of this Convention." Article 5 (d) viii specified "the right to freedom of opinion and expression" and 5 (d) ix "the right to freedom of peaceful assembly and association." We passed the second amendment to the Swedes, who helpfully put it forth as their own. As we expected, the sponsors rejected the U.S. amendment, but accepted the "Swedish" amendment, which made it possible for us to vote for the resolution, adopted unanimously.

When the convention came up for a vote in Plenary on December 21, 1965, Justice Goldberg stated clearly and explicitly that the United States would be guided by the First Amendment to its constitution in interpreting any and all parts of the convention. The convention came into force on January 4, 1969. The United States has not become a party to the convention, but our maneuver spared us the embarrassment of opposing a convention against racial discrimination while preserving our First Amendment position.

THE PUEBLO INCIDENT, NUCLEAR NONPROLIFERATION, AND OUTER SPACE

Goldberg and the United Nations again proved useful to American policy in January 1968, when North Korea seized the USS *Pueblo*. According to U.S. evidence, the *Pueblo* was seized on January 23 at least thirteen miles offshore, which would have put it in international waters even by North Korean standards. Secretary Rusk denounced the seizure as an act of war, and feelings in the United States were running high. The Joint Chiefs of Staff recommended a military strike to liberate the *Pueblo* and its crew, but Goldberg, with Rusk's support, persuaded President Johnson to use the United Nations as an escape valve to allow emotions to be vented against North Korea's action. Johnson, who had his hands full in Vietnam, was not eager to undertake another military action, yet the seizure could not be ignored.

At the Security Council Goldberg presented a strong case, using detailed maps to show that the *Pueblo* had definitely been in international waters. The debates were carried live on television, so that the American public did not have a sense of inaction. And while the debates were going on, Hungary's permanent representative to the UN, who unofficially represented North Korea as well, received word from North Korea to communicate to Goldberg that they were prepared to negotiate the release of the crew.[39]

Parallel with the diplomatic effort at the UN, Johnson had ordered a strong naval buildup in the Sea of Japan, called up 14,000 navy and air force reservists, and alerted and reinforced land-based tactical air units in South Korea. The Soviets countered with a naval buildup of their own and a strongly worded warning to the United States not to use military force. As a result of the channel of communication opened through the Hungarian ambassador at the UN, the United States by early February requested closed meetings with Korea at Panmunjom, and on February 6 the carrier *Enterprise* was sent south and away from Korea, signaling the abandonment of any military options. The Soviet military buildup was also halted.

The negotiations at Panmunjom did, in fact, lead to the release of the crew of 83, after eleven months. Thus, although the conditions were onerous, the main American objective was achieved—and peacefully.

Despite this success, by February 1968 Goldberg's relations with the President began to sour. The Viet Cong–North Vietnamese Tet offensive that month was a shattering defeat for the United States and South Vietnam, with huge losses of lives, and it brought home to Goldberg the futility of his efforts to help end the war through either the UN Security Council or the secretary general. Johnson, on his side, was dismayed by the U.S. failure in Vietnam under his presidency, and this did not help his disposition. When arrangements were finally concluded for four-party negotiations (the United States, South Vietnam, North Vietnam, and the Viet Cong) in Paris, Johnson chose Averell Harriman and Cyrus Vance as his representatives. This must have been a bitter blow to Goldberg, who had made his reputation as a negotiator and had accepted the UN post in large part because he hoped thereby to help bring about a peaceful settlement in Vietnam.

Goldberg would have resigned in early 1968; however, President Johnson asked him to postpone his resignation long enough to guide the Nuclear Non-proliferation Treaty (NPT) to endorsement by the UN General Assembly.[40] The treaty had been under consideration for several years. On November 23, 1965, the General Assembly adopted, by a vote of 93 to 0, with 5 abstentions, a resolution setting forth the principles on which the treaty should be based.[41] In 1966 both superpowers began to work in earnest on a formula for a treaty. But they were deterred from assuming a joint initiative by one stubborn problem, that of inspection. The Soviet Union favored the International Atomic Energy Agency (IAEA) as the main inspection organ for the treaty, whereas the United States, under pressure from the western European countries, preferred the European Atomic Energy Community (EURATOM) as the inspection organ for its European allies.

Since both countries felt that a nonproliferation treaty was urgently needed, they set to work to overcome their differences. The Soviets' concern was heightened after China became the fifth nuclear power, and the specter of a potential German nuclear power was particularly disturbing to them. On August 24, 1967, after intensive secret negotiations, the USSR and the United States submitted separate but identical drafts in the Eighteen Nation Disarmament Committee (ENDC), leaving blank the article that was to embody the inspection provision.

In the ENDC a number of nonnuclear powers objected to the draft on the grounds that it did not provide adequately for their security. After lengthy negotiations the two superpowers, presenting a common front, managed to get an agreed report to the General Assembly on March 14, 1968. In the meantime, they also overcame their one remaining difference on inspection. It was agreed that the IAEA verification procedures would ultimately apply to all nonnuclear states but that EURATOM would have an inspection role for its members during a transitional period.

Goldberg had participated briefly but effectively in the ENDC negotiations with the nonnuclear states, supplementing the efforts of William H. Foster, who represented the United States at the ENDC. He so impressed Vasily Kuznetzov, the Soviet first deputy foreign minister, that the latter asked Goldberg to take the lead in negotiating General Assembly approval in New York.[42]

In the Assembly many specific reservations were proposed by nonnuclear states of Asia, Africa, and Latin America, seeking stronger guarantees and expressing displeasure at what they perceived as a double standard. Their objections were met in part when the superpowers agreed to provide security assurances to the nonnuclear powers through a formal Security Council resolution.

Finally, on June 12, 1968, the General Assembly endorsed the treaty to halt the spread of nuclear weapons. The vote was 95 in favor, 4 against, 21 abstentions, and 4 not voting.[43] On June 19, 1968, the three nuclear powers on the Security Council gave their formal pledge to assist any nonnuclear country that was threatened by nuclear aggression. A resolution in the council welcoming these pledges of assistance was passed by a vote of 10 in favor and 0 against, with 5 abstentions (Algeria, Brazil, France, India, and Pakistan).[44]

Goldberg could well be proud of his role in securing this endorsement. The Soviet and American delegations worked closely together and lobbied hard for the endorsement, but Goldberg was the leader in persuasion and negotiation of the compromises that made the endorsement possible. He resigned shortly after the successful conclusion of the NPT exercise.

He had accomplished a great deal—resolving the Article 19 crisis, helping to bring about a cease-fire in the India-Pakistan fighting, negotiating cease-fires and resolution 242 in the Middle East crisis of 1967, bringing U.S. positions closer to African objectives in Southwest Africa and Rhodesia, helping to settle the *Pueblo* crisis, and playing a key role in the negotiation of the Nuclear Nonproliferation Treaty and the treaty banning the stationing of weapons of mass destruction in outer space. But he had not been able to get the UN to help bring peace in Vietnam, for reasons completely beyond his control, nor to bring about a resolution of the dispute over Chinese representation. On the principle of universality, he favored having all divided states in the UN—North and South Vietnam, North and South Korea, East and West Germany, and the two Chinas—but the key nations involved were not ready for such a solution.

Goldberg felt great bitterness about the way he had been treated by President Johnson. He deeply regretted having left the court under pressure from Johnson. He resented the fact that Johnson resumed bombing every time there appeared to be hope of peace negotiations brokered by the secretary general of the UN. At one point, he calculated that the average cost of killing a Viet Cong would have provided enough to afford the latter a lifetime on the French Riviera. He was particularly offended that Johnson did not choose him to represent the United States when negotiations on peace with North Vietnam finally began. After all, he was known for his superb negotiation skills. He left a bitter man, but his accomplishments as Permanent Representative were extraordinary and of enormous value to the United States, Israel, and world peace.

Goldberg went on to become a partner in the prestigious law firm of Paul, Weiss, Rifkind, Wharton, and Garrison in New York. Then he moved back to Washington and established his own practice. In one case he represented Curt Flood, outfielder with the St. Louis Cardinals, who had played out his contract and wanted to be a free agent, to sell his services to the highest bidder. The Cardinals refused, citing the "reserve clause," which tied a player to the team that hired him until they were ready to trade him. Flood's case came before the U.S. Supreme Court, which ruled that the "reserve clause" was an unreasonable restraint of trade, contrary to the fourteenth Amendment to the U.S. Constitution. As a result, baseball players who complete their contract can now become free agents, a major increase in their bargaining power. Goldberg's skill as a lawyer and his status as a former justice were certainly important pluses for Flood.

When Goldberg died, we held memorial services for him at the U.S. Mission to the UN. I delivered the eulogy and could pay a sincere tribute to a most remarkable and dedicated man.

BALL AND WIGGINS

Goldberg's resignation came with seven months left in the Johnson administration. To fill the gap the President persuaded George W. Ball, former undersecretary of state in the Kennedy and the early Johnson administration, to take over.

Ball had never shown much interest in the UN, even while his old friend Adlai Stevenson had been the permanent representative. He had headed the U.S. delegation to the UN Conference on Trade and Development in 1964, where he decided to show the less developed countries that the United States could be firm. In his own words:

I felt compelled to tell [UNCTAD] that what they were seeking was not politically feasible. Labor-intensive industries in the United States were then pressing hard for restrictions on imports from the less developed countries, using the old argument about the unfair advantages of cheap labor. Refutable as it was by the rational answers we persistently gave, the "cheap labor" contention always found strong resonance in the Congress. Since we were, thus, hard pressed to resist discriminatory restrictions against imports from the poor countries, it was quite impracticable to propose that we encourage those imports by preferential treatment. Although I disappointed the UNCTAD Conference and no doubt created the impression that I was indifferent to the predicament of the poor countries—which was far from the truth—it would have been a great disservice had we raised expectations we could not fulfill.[45]

While I believe candor is admirable on most occasions and generally admire George Ball greatly, I think he was wrong at UNCTAD. The United States, by staking out negative positions on this and other objectives of the less developed countries, became the lightning rod for all their frustrations.

On the other hand, Ball alone among President Johnson's high-level advisers openly took the negative on Vietnam. In October 1964, after the Tonkin Gulf incident but before massive American intervention, he wrote a hundred-page memorandum advocating a withdrawal from the "gluepot" of Indochina or, if that could not be done, at least a concentration upon the ground war in South Vietnam itself rather than "going North" with air power. In the fall of 1961 Ball had warned President Kennedy against a commitment in Vietnam.[46]

Ball had many other admirable qualities. He was a man of broad knowledge and experience, with a keen analytical mind, a good sense of humor, and a likable, outgoing personality. He was also the most articulate man I have ever met. I have seen him dictate into a recorder the complete text of a lengthy statement, which would come out not only logical, coherent, and well organized, but also well styled and with good syntax. Naturally, he was superb with ad lib statements in the Security Council.

In the one test that came during his brief tenure, the Soviet invasion of

Czechoslovakia, Ball did an outstanding job. When the issue came before the Security Council in August 1968, he was brilliant in his presentation of the case against the aggression by the Soviet Union and its Warsaw Pact partners. The Soviet representative, Fedorenko, opposed even inscription of the item, arguing that his was an internal matter for the "socialist" (communist) countries that should not be discussed in the Council (as the United States had argued that its intervention in the Dominican Republic crisis of 1965 was a matter for the OAS, not the UN Security Council). After inscription, Fedorenko contended that the Soviet forces had been "invited" into Czechoslovakia, but he had difficulty in specifying who issued the invitation. He also used what came to be known as the Brezhnev doctrine—that fraternal socialist countries should intervene whenever one of their number was threatened by a counterrevolution.[47] Beyond that, Fedorenko repeatedly filibustered into the wee hours of the morning, hoping to stretch out the Council's consideration of the item until Czech Prime Minister Dubcek, then in Moscow, could either be pressured into requesting that the item be removed from the agenda or be replaced by someone who would. Ball was just as determined to keep the proceedings going until a resolution could be brought to a vote.

Tactically, at least, the West won. On Saturday, August 22, Foreign Minister Jiri Hayek appeared at the Council. He looked straight across the room at Fedorenko and declared: "No one in the government of Czechoslovakia invited your troops; no one wanted your troops." That same afternoon the Council voted on a draft resolution presented by Brazil, Canada, Denmark, France, Paraguay, the United Kingdom, and the United States condemning the invasion and calling upon the USSR and its allies to withdraw forthwith. The vote was 10 in favor, 2 against (Hungary and the Soviet Union), and 3 abstentions (Algeria, India, and Pakistan). Because the Soviet Union is a permanent member of the Security Council, its negative vote constituted a veto.

I have often heard people argue that the UN could become much more effective if Article 27 of the Charter were amended to remove the veto. I disagree. In this instance, even if the resolution had been declared adopted, would the Soviets have obeyed? If they refused, how could they be forced out without starting World War III? And how many in the West would have wanted another great war? What was required here was a Soviet willingness to go along with the majority view, not a procedural change.

Of course, we knew in advance that the Soviets would veto the resolution. Why work for days and nights to arrive at a veto? The United States was not prepared to use force in Czechoslovakia, yet the Soviet aggression could not be ignored. The matter had to be fully aired in the Security Council and the Soviets forced to pay a price at least in world public opinion for their brutal suppression in Czechoslovakia. And pay they did. A number of Western communist leaders opposed the aggression, and Peking denounced the Brezhnev doctrine as a manifesto of "socialist imperialism."[48] Clearly, China feared that Moscow might wish to assure the purity of the communist faith in China by a similar military intervention. Yugoslavia and Romania opposed the Brezhnev doctrine for similar reasons.

Referring to these fears, George Ball later wrote:

I was acutely aware of their apprehensions, since as ambassador to the UN at the time, I spent long hours with the Yugoslavs and with the Romanian Foreign Minister. It gave them little comfort to reflect that Soviet intervention would be undertaken in the same spirit of "fraternal solicitude" Moscow had shown other socialist republics. They knew only too well the meaning of that term; it was the same kind of fraternal solicitude Cain had shown his brother Abel.[49]

Following the Soviet veto, the United States consulted with friendly delegations from around the world as to next steps. We gave serious consideration to inscribing the Czech item on the agenda of the twenty-third session of the UN General Assembly that opened the next month. We did not do so because virtually all of the Western European countries thought such a move would be counterproductive, especially since the Soviets had installed a puppet regime that would represent Czechoslovakia in the Assembly. Denunciations of the Soviet action were made, of course, in the Assembly's general debate.

In September, Ball resigned to campaign for Hubert Humphrey in the 1968 presidential election. He detested Richard Nixon, as had his friend Adlai Stevenson, and he could not rest with the thought that he would stand aside while there was still a chance of defeating Nixon.

Ball's successor was James Russell Wiggins, editor of the *Washington Post*. Russ Wiggins knew he would have the job for only a few months, but he was retiring from the *Post* anyway and accepted the UN assignment to help Lyndon Johnson, his friend. There were no crises during his tenure; the most startling development was the announcement that Jacqueline Kennedy would marry Aristotle Onassis. That afternoon, he stuck his head inside my door and gave me the news. He added, "As an old newsman, I can tell you, if you had any foul deeds to commit, tonight's the night, it won't get in the papers." On another occasion, we were sitting in the General Assembly Hall when Jamil Baroody, who represented Saudi Arabia, started his statement by saying, "Let us get to the genesis of this matter." Russ turned to me and said, "When Baroody starts on genesis, it's time for exodus." And we left.

Out of deep conviction and concern, Wiggins strongly supported the Swedish initiative to hold a UN conference on environment. He was an altogether delightful man, well informed, experienced, wise, and extraordinarily good-natured.

NOTES

1. *New York Times Sunday Magazine*, February 6, 1966, p. 16.
2. Arnold Beichman, *The "Other" State Department, The United States Mission to the United Nations: Its Role in the Making of Foreign Policy* (New York: Basic Books, 1967), p. 114.
3. Dorothy K. Goldberg, *A Private View of a Public Life* (New York: Charterhouse, 1975), pp. 193-94.
4. Ibid., p. 195.
5. Goldberg acceptance statement at the White House, July 20, 1965, in *The Defenses of Freedom—The Public Papers of Arthur J. Goldberg*, ed. Daniel Patrick Moynihan (New York: Harper & Row, 1966), p. xv.
6. Ibid., p. 5. Address to the Conference on World Peace through Law, Washington, D.C., September 17, 1965.
7. Ibid., p. 65.
8. Norman Cousins, "Journeys with Humphrey," *Saturday Review*, March 4, 1978, pp. 11-14.
9. Walter W. Rostow, *The Diffusion of Power* (New York: Macmillan, 1972), pp. 358-60.
10. Lyndon B. Johnson, *The Vantage Point: Perspectives of the Presidency 1963-69* (New York: Holt, Rinehart & Winston, 1971), pp. 543-45.
11. Goldberg, *A Private View of a Public Life*, p. 223.
12. Louis B. Fleming, *Los Angeles Times-Mirror*, July 17, 1966.
13. Beichman, *The "Other" State Department*, pp. 145-46.
14. Goldberg, *A Private View of a Public Life*, p. 224.
15. Beichman, *The "Other" State Department*, p. 174.
16. USUN press release 4615, August 16, 1965, pp. 3-4.
17. S.C. Res. S/211, September 20, 1965, and S.C. Res. S/215, November 5, 1965.
18. Ruth B. Russell, *The United Nations and United States Security Policy* (Washington, D.C.: Brookings Institution, 1968), p. 187.
19. G.A. Res. 2012 (XX), October 12, 1965.
20. G.A. Res. 2024 (XX), November 11, 1965.
21. S.C. Res. S/216, November 12, 1965 and S.C. Res. S/217, November 20, 1965. Res. S/217 called for an embargo on the shipment of oil to Rhodesia.
22. See Anthony Lake, *The "Tar Baby" Option* (New York: Columbia University Press, 1976), pp. 62-122, for a full account of the U.S. policy toward Rhodesia, Goldberg's role in it, and the impact of the sanctions.
23. U.S. State Department press release 304, December 29, 1966, pp. 6-7.
24. S.C. Res. S/253 (1968).
25. Lake, *The "Tar Baby" Option*, see also Chapter IX of this volume.
26. Drew Middleton, *New York Times*, July 26, 1977.
27. Arthur S. Lall, *The United Nations and the Middle East Crisis, 1967* (New York: Columbia University Press, 1967), pp. 8-19.
28. Nasser interview with Eric Rouieau in *Le Monde*, Paris, February 19, 1970.
29. For U Thant's rationale, see S.C. Doc S 7906, May 26, 1967, paragraphs 1-8.

30. S.C. Doc. S/7925, June 2, 1967.
31. S.C. Doc. S/7906, May 26, 1967, paragraph 14.
32. Rostow, *The Diffusion of Power*, pp. 417–19.
33. UN Security Council document S/7951/Rev.2.
34. Lall, *The United Nations and the Middle East Crisis*, pp. 46–115, provides a lucid, carefully documented, and detailed account of the Security Council's proceedings in June, to which I am indebted. Lall's appendix includes the texts of all relevant resolutions and draft resolutions. For an account of the Soviet and U.S. roles during private negotiations, see my statement in *The Big Powers and the Present Crisis in the Middle East*, ed. Samuel Merlin, (Cranbury, N.J.: Associated University Presses, 1970), pp. 92–140.
35. See G.A. Doc. A/L.572/Rev. 3 and G.A. Doc. A/L523/Rev.1, fifth emergency session of the General Assembly.
36. Dorothy Goldberg, *A Private View of a Public Life*, p. 250, writes that the "concept and language were Arthur's work"; this corresponds to my own recollections.
37. Subsequently Lord Caradon confirmed that omission of "all" and "the" in the phrase "from occupied territories" was deliberate and expressed his own interpretation of resolution 242 to mean that Israel should withdraw to "*secure and recognized boundaries*" [italics mine]. Lord Caradon, "Is Peace Possible" in S.M. Finger, ed., *The New World Balance and Peace in the Middle East* (New York: Associated Universities Press, 1975), p. 221. See also Lall, *The United Nations and the Middle East Crisis*, p. 254, for confirmation that Caradon rejected an Arab effort to use the term "all the territories" in resolution 242.
38. Lall, *The United Nations and the Middle East Crisis*, pp. 208–10, states that the text agreed to by the United States and the USSR was based on a new Latin American draft. See also Security Council records of debate on November 17 (S/PV/1373).
39. Rostow, *The Diffusion of Power*, p. 419.
40. Goldberg, *A Private View of a Public Life*, pp. 250.
41. Ibid., pp. 250–51.
42. Ibid., p. 250. Mrs. Goldberg writes that the Nonproliferation Treaty was the achievement in her husband's UN career "in which our family takes the most pride."
43. G.A. Res. 2373, June 12, 1968.
44. S.C. Res. 255, June 19, 1968.
45. George W. Ball, *Diplomacy for a Crowded World* (Boston: Atlantic–Little, Brown, 1976), p. 282.
46. Tom Wicker, *JFK and LBJ: The Influence of Personality upon Politics* (New York: Morrow, 1968), p. 249.
47. Ibid., p. 269.
48. In Brezhnev's words, "The sovereignty of each socialist country cannot be opposed to the world of socialism of the world revolutionary movement." From "Sovereignty and International Duties of Socialist Countries," *Pravda*, September 25, 1968, as translated in Ivo Duchacek, *Nations and Men*, 3d ed. (Hinsdale, Ill.: Dryden, 1975), p. 424.
49. Ball, *Diplomacy for a Crowded World*, p. 107.

CHAPTER X

Charles Yost and the Nixon-Kissinger Years

Charles Yost, who became the U.S. permanent representative in January 1969, was the first career diplomat to serve in the post. Yost was, in fact, the "professional's professional." Entering the Foreign Service as a young man, he rose through the ranks to the top grade, career ambassador. This is a rank held at any given time by only ten to twelve outstanding diplomats. He served with distinction in Eastern Europe, the Middle East, and the Far East, and the State Department before becoming ambassador, successively, to Laos, Syria, and Morocco. Soft-spoken, slight in build, and given to understatement, Yost had a professional diplomat's caution about emotionally charged language and belief in quiet diplomacy rather than spectacular public confrontation. Yet he was as firm as a rock on principle and relentlessly logical, incisive, and realistic in analyzing situations. Goldberg's deputy, James Nabrit, referred to Yost as "the most stubborn quiet man I ever met."

Yost brought other unusual qualifications to the job. He had worked closely with Edward Stettinius and Adlai Stevenson at the founding conference of the UN in San Francisco in 1945. Stevenson was so much impressed with him that he asked Yost to become his deputy for the UN Security Council in 1961. Yost was then ambassador to Morocco, with all the perquisites of a chief of mission overseas—residence, servants, car, chauffeur, and generous allowances—none of which he would have at USUN. Nevertheless, he accepted, because of his deep and sustained belief in the importance of the UN and his high regard for Adlai Stevenson.

I recall lunching with Yost while he was still weighing Stevenson's offer.

We had known each other in Laos, where he was the ambassador and I was chief of the political section in 1955–1956. When he raised the question, I told him that his coming to the USUN would be a personal sacrifice, given the grueling schedule and the loss of perquisites, but it would be a great thing for the United States. Knowing Yost, I am sure that our lunch conversation was mainly a matter of renewing friendship and that his mind had already been made up. In any case, he came to USUN and remained there from early 1961 to his retirement from the Foreign Service in 1966, earning the highest praise from both Stevenson and Goldberg.

Yost devoted the next two years, 1966–1968, to research and writing at Columbia University, the UN Association of the United States, and the Council on Foreign Relations. However, as noted in Chapter IX, there was a brief interlude in May 1967 when he went to Egypt at President Johnson's request in an effort to avert war in the Middle East. Yost was the author of innumerable classified think pieces for the State Department as well as many published articles and three thoughtful books on foreign policy and the human condition: *The Age of Triumph and Frustration* (1964), *The Insecurity of Nations* (1968), and *The Conduct and Misconduct of Foreign Affairs* (1972).

Yet President Nixon did not pick Yost because he shared a deep belief in the UN or desired to strengthen the organization. On the contrary, Nixon had a generally negative attitude toward the UN. For political reasons he wanted a Democrat in his cabinet. Although the UN post carried cabinet status, he considered it of little real importance. Initially he offered the post to Hubert Humphrey, whom he had just defeated in the presidential race. Humphrey declined, as Nixon must have expected he would. He then approached Sergeant Shriver, former President Kennedy's brother-in-law. Shriver expressed great interest but stated certain conditions for acceptance. Among other things, he required a pledge that federal poverty programs would not be cut. Nixon then told Secretary Designate Rogers to inform Shriver he had decided against him because he found it "intolerable to have a prospective ambassadorial appointee making demands relating to domestic policy."[1] Then the job was offered to Yost, who had supported Humphrey's campaign but was essentially a career diplomat rather than a political figure.

Some insight was provided by Arthur Goldberg, at a lunch we had in early 1971, after George Bush had succeeded Yost. Goldberg told me Nixon had phoned him to get his views about a Yost appointment. Goldberg replied: "You won't have as much trouble with him as Lyndon Johnson had with me." Goldberg said he knew that was what was on Nixon's mind.

It is significant that in his memoirs of 1,090 pages, *RN*, Nixon does not mention Yost even once. George Bush is not mentioned in his UN capacity either. John Scali, the third and last Nixon appointee, is mentioned only in connection with the Yom Kippur War in October 1973, as reporting developments in the UN Security Council. Significantly, the UN is not mentioned even once during the long section of Nixon's memoirs covering his vice presidency.

Yost himself was under no illusions. When I interviewed him in 1978 he said he knew from the outset that Nixon had a negative attitude toward the UN. Nevertheless, he accepted the post, believing that Nixon might otherwise have chosen someone hostile toward the UN.

Moreover, Nixon's principal adviser on foreign policy was Henry Kissinger, presidential assistant for national security affairs. Kissinger, an outstanding advocate of realpolitik and balance-of-power politics,[2] had no more respect for the UN than Nixon did. Samuel de Palma, Assistant Secretary of State for International Organization Affairs during 1969–1973, recalls being told by Kissinger: "Don't bother me with that UN crap."[3] De Palma says that, on occasions when Kissinger did not want to be bothered, his deputy, General Haig, was conscientious about seeing that critical issues at the UN were at least brought to the President's notice. Kissinger and Nixon concentrated on great-power relationships.

By contract, Yost considered balance-of-power politics a failure. In *The Insecurity of Nations* he writes: "The system of national egotism, armaments, alliances, balance of power, deterrence, challenge and response has brought no security to its strongest proponents, to Germany, to Russia, to France, to Britain, to Italy, to Japan, to China. It had brought temporary security to the United States only because this country has hitherto been protected by distance and allies, but even the United States is now subject to the loss of half its population in a few hours." He notes that the military power of the United States has increased vastly since 1949 while its national security has been rapidly diminishing. He believes that "great power may be fully as hazardous as great weakness. . . . National power, even relatively disinterested power, inevitably provokes fear and eventually more-or-less matching counterforce. Uncontrolled national power, moreover, creates in those who possess it an almost irresistible temptation to use it; but its use, even for seemingly legitimate ends, provokes still more fear and still more counterforce. The law of disproportionate response, triggered by such fears, quickly takes over." He concludes: "The inherent insecurity of nations in the modern environment is such that there may be no safety for mankind except in a fundamental reform, as early suppression of the nation-state system."[4]

Yet Yost had few illusions about the UN. He noted that it has no standing armed force, no decisive power to control national armaments, limit national conflict, or enforce peaceful settlements.[5] The Security Council is often immobilized by great power antagonisms and the veto. The General Assembly can only recommend to governments, not order; the "sovereign equality" of its members and the influx of ministates progressively dims its reflection of real power and, hence, the impact of its recommendations; and "the preoccupation of its more numerous and least powerful members with the vestigial problems of colonialism distracts it wastefully from the major problems of today and tomorrow."[6]

Nixon and Kissinger would certainly agree with this catalog of weaknesses. The difference is that they considered the weaknesses a reason for ignoring the UN on most major political and security issues, at least for four years and nine months, that is, until the Yom Kippur War, when the UN became an important element in separating Arab and Israeli forces. Yost, on the other hand, considered the weaknesses an agenda for reforming and strengthening the UN. This should be effected by the restoration of great power cooperation, primarily in the gradual reinforcement of multilateral peacekeeping through the United Nations. In *The Insecurity of Nations* he concludes: "The revival and reinforcement of the United Nations no doubt seems, and at the moment may be, Utopian. The point to be made again and again, to be hammered unmercifully into our proud, bad, silly heads, is that the attempt to achieve the security of nations by national means under modern circumstances is still more Utopian."[7]

Yost's inability to convince Nixon and Kissinger on measures to strengthen the UN was a foregone conclusion. His influence on policy was reduced even further by the weakness of the secretary of state's position in Nixon's foreign policy councils. Nixon had appointed William P. Rogers as an old and trusted friend whose open, low-key manner might help in dealing with Congress, not as a man whose judgment on foreign policy was to be valued. It soon became apparent that the President's principal adviser on foreign affairs was Kissinger, not the secretary of state. Yost, having no clout with either the President or Kissinger, had to work through the State Department and its chief, who himself had little impact.

Even when Rogers signed a memorandum to the President at the behest of Yost or Assistant Secretary de Palma, he would not fight for it if the President disagreed. De Palma recalls drafting a memorandum for the secretary's signature recommending against a cut in the U.S. contribution to the UN Educational, Scientific, and Cultural Organization (UNESCO). There was no formal reply; the President simply wrote on a corner of the memorandum: "To hell with this outfit. Let's gut it. RMN."[8]

When asked what issues he had been able to exert an influence on, Yost replied: "One percent and the high commissioner for human rights."[9] This was a shorthand way of indicating that the U.S. delegation had been authorized to vote for a 1970 resolution on the second United Nations Development Decade and to support a Costa Rican proposal to establish a high commissioner for human rights. These were, as Yost would be the first to acknowledge, marginal achievements. In fact, as we shall see in discussing specific issues, Yost was able to exercise a constructive influence on a number of issues, but none was of decisive importance. The further an issue from the vital concerns of Nixon and Kissinger, the more likely Yost was to have an impact.

The obverse of this observation is illustrated by Yost's role on the Middle East, which was of prime concern to Nixon and Kissinger. Throughout 1969 and the early part of 1970, Yost was engaged in four-power talks at the UN with the representatives of Britain, France, and the Soviet Union. When these talks became more serious than Kissinger wanted them to be and the Soviets endeavored to get into terms of settlement, Yost was instructed to slow up the process.[10] In fairness to Nixon it should be noted that the Soviet proposals would have had the major powers make judgments on boundaries (total Israeli withdrawal) and impose them on the parties. The United States, while taking the position that any changes in the prewar borders should be "insubstantial," held that a durable peace agreement must be negotiated by the parties themselves, as provided in Security Council Resolution 242.[11]

Conversely, Yost was able to gain State Department and White House support for a more flexible position on guidelines for future UN peacekeeping operations, which did not cut across any vital current Nixon/Kissinger concern. Negotiations had started in the aftermath of the Article 19 crisis over the refusal of the Soviets to pay their share of the costs of UN peacekeeping operations in the Congo and the Middle East. At first the United States had encouraged the middle-sized and smaller powers to come forward with guidelines to assure better preparation and more reliable financing of future operations. This effort foundered on the rock of unyielding Soviet and French opposition. Then, encouraged by the other members of the Special Committee on Peacekeeping Operations, the United States undertook intensive negotiations with the Soviet representatives in an effort to agree on guidelines.[12]

The exercise was a USUN initiative from the outset, but there was constant consultation with Assistant Secretary de Palma and his special assistant, Nathan Pelcovits. To accommodate the Soviets, we started discussions on a model that would fit even their restrictive interpretation of the Charter, that is, "UN Military observers established or authorized by the Security Council for observation purposes pursuant to Council resolutions." Discussion began in a Working Group of eight countries, consisting of the four officers of the committee (Mexico, Canada, Czechoslovakia, and Egypt) and the Big Four (Britain, France, the Soviet Union, and the United States). In 49 meetings, the Working Group agreed on five of the eight chapters envisaged for the model. Of the remaining three chapters, financial and legal arrangements did not present serious obstacles; the major obstacle was the chapter on direction and control. The Soviets wanted all operations directly under the control of the Security Council, where they have the veto. The United States acknowledged the ultimate authority of the Council but held that day-to-day operations and implementing decisions should be delegated to the secretary general. Our negotiations in 1970, largely carried out between Ambassador Lev Mendelevich of the USSR and me, were aimed at finding an acceptable division of responsibilities between the Council and the secretary general. Personal relations between Mendelevich and me were excellent. At one point where he conceived a possible compromise, he asked me to seek Washington approval so that it might appear as an American initiative. After receiving tentative State Department clearance to accept the compromise as a basis for discussion, Yost arranged a meeting with Ambassador Malik (USSR) at USUN, with Mendelevich and me present. Malik, with the compromise formula in front of him as an "American" suggestion, asked me to explain it. I had to do so with a straight face while Mendelevich sat there with an equally straight face. It looked as if we might reach agreement; however, Moscow's approval never came. Yost was a great source of strength and support throughout the negotiations. He fully approved of the Soviet-U.S. effort to strengthen peacekeeping, understood the Soviet position completely, and was willing to push Washington to make reasonable concessions in an effort to reach agreement. His views were highly respected in the State Department, and his telegrams recommending various adjustments in the U.S. position were most effective. In fact, the presidential stamp of approval was given to our efforts. In his report to the Congress on February 25, 1971, Nixon stated that "a crucial development would be joint recognition by the United States and the Soviet Union of a common interest in strengthening the UN's peacekeeping capacity. A major effort should be made to reach an agreement on reliable ground rules for peacekeeping operations."[13]

Unfortunately, the gap was never bridged. Yet the effort eventually paid off in a completely unforeseen way. Following a cease-fire in the 1973 Yom Kippur War, the Security Council, in resolution 340 of October 25, 1973, decided "to set up immediately under its authority a United Nations Emergency Force to be composed of personnel drawn from states members of the United Nations except the Permanent Members of the Security Council." At the Council's request the secretary general prepared a report setting out the force's terms of reference, proposed plan of action, estimated costs, and method of financing.[14]

According to reliable sources in the UN Secretariat, this document was drafted in the light of proposals and statements made over many years in the Special Committee on Peacekeeping Operations and its Working Group. Remarkably, the secretary general's document avoids seriously offending any major power, incorporates all elements agreed upon, and draws up a modus operandi in which all powers can acquiesce even though they would not specifically endorse some of its features. This technique has been particularly important in the establishment, command, and control of the operations. Consequently, the future of peacekeeping might be better served by using UNEF II as a model or precedent, as in common law, rather than to attempt to codify guidelines.

Specific clauses in the secretary general's document demonstrate its achievements and advantages as a precedent. First, it states "that the force will be under the command of the United Nations, vested in the secretary-general, under the authority of the Security Council. The command in the field will be exercised by a Force Commander appointed by the secretary-general with the consent of the Security Council. The Commander will be responsible to the secretary-general." This brief paragraph skillfully overcomes some of the main problems encountered in the Working Group of the Committee on Peacekeeping by clearly giving the secretary general a mandate to run UNEF operations on a day-to-day basis and to appoint a force commander, both of which duties were resisted by the USSR in negotiations on general guidelines.

Second, paragraph 3(c) of the secretary general's document states that "the Force will be composed of a number of contingents to be provided by selected countries, *upon the request of the secretary-general*" (italics mine). The Soviets had argued that the Security Council should make the request. The paragraph continues: "The contingents will be selected in consultation with the Security Council and with the parties concerned, bearing in mind the accepted principle of equitable geographic representation." To "bear in mind" equitable geographic representation is less rigid than the preferred Soviet version stating that "it is important to *base it* on the accepted principle of equitable geographic distribution" (italics mine).

Third, this document also indicates in its proposed plan of action that the secretary general is to appoint the commander of the emergency force as soon as possible, with the consent of the Security Council. The secretary general had already appointed the chief of staff of UNTSO, Major General Siilasvuo, as interim commander of the force. I can recall months of unsuccessful negotiations with the USSR, during our efforts to develop general guidelines, over this question of what should be done in an emergency before the secretary general could consult the Security Council about the commander. Here the problem is resolved in one brief paragraph.

Finally, the closing paragraph of the secretary general's document stipulates that "the costs of the Force shall be considered as expenses of the Organization to be borne by the Members in accordance with Article 17, paragraph 2, of the Charter." The USSR was long reluctant to agree that the General Assembly could make assessments for peacekeeping under the provisions of this article.

In these important respects the secretary general's document represents a practical answer to the real problems of running a peacekeeping force. It is apparently easier for the USSR to acquiesce in these provisions in a particular case than to endorse them as general principles or guidelines. That is why a "common-law" precedent approach may be better than an attempt at codification. The establishment of UNDOF, a UN Force on the Golan Heights, in 1974, and of the UN Interim Force in Lebanon (UNIFIL) in 1978, on the same general criteria as UNEF II, reinforces the precedent. Yet it is doubtful that the secretary general's recommendations would have been accepted with so little difficulty had it not been for the long negotiations on guidelines that clarified the limits of tolerance of the USSR and the United States and induced both of them to consider carefully during 1969–1971 the problems that would be faced in finding a mutually acceptable formula.[15] Concerned about the fate of American prisoners of war in Vietnam, the United Sates initiated a resolution on the rights of POWs in the Assembly's Third Committee. As the delegation's troubleshooter, I was assigned to the item along with Senator Claiborne Pell, who made our official statement introducing the resolution.

Knowing the resolution would have tough sledding because of its unstated but implied relationship to Vietnam, we organized a cosponsor group with wide geographic distribution: Belgium, Dahomey, Dominican Republic, Greece, Haiti, Italy, Malagasy Republic, New Zealand, Philippines, Thailand, and Togo. Brazil's delegation had tentatively agreed to cosponsor but did not receive the necessary instructions from its government. At a delegation meeting, Senator Pell expressed concern about having as cosponsors dictatorships like Brazil and Greece. I pointed out that democracies were in the minority in the UN membership, that wide sponsorship would be crucial to success, that Brazil had standing among the Latin Americans, and that cosponsorship on one issue did not imply approval of everything a government did. Senator Javits supported this position. He told Pell that when he was working for progress on civil rights in the U.S. Senate he would welcome support on such an issue from the most reactionary southern senator. That swung the delegation.

As expected, the resolution was strongly opposed by the Soviet Union and its supporters, which characterized the U.S. initiative as a political move designed to gain support for one side in the Vietnam War. The USSR also tried to depict the resolution as a tactic against national liberation movements such as those in Africa. Nevertheless, despite repeated assaults, the resolution was adopted in the Third Committee on December 1, 1970. The General Assembly approved it on December 9 by a vote of 67 to 30, with 20 abstentions.[16] The wide cosponsorship was undoubtedly a key factor. Adoption of the resolution had no demonstrable effect on Hanoi's treatment of American prisoners of war, but once the President had raised this issue, failure in the General Assembly would have had repercussions in the Congress and on the American public.

No such success met U.S. efforts on colonial issues. From the birth of the UN the United States had generally had greater sympathy for self-determination in Asia and Africa than its Western European allies who were colonial powers there. As these issues were brought to the United

Nations, USUN had a consistently greater sympathy than Washington. USUN's voting constituency at the UN had an increasingly large majority of anticolonial states; naturally, USUN did not wish to antagonize this majority on those questions, since it needed their votes on other issues. Washington, on the other hand, thought in national security terms; it attached greater importance to relations with its NATO partners, such as Britain, France, Belgium, and Portugal. Such tension was normally worked out through consultation and compromise. On some issues—that of Indonesia in 1946–1949, Suez in 1956, and the Congo in 1960—the final U.S. position came down against NATO partners for reasons of overall national interest. More often the alliance interest prevailed. In 1960, for example, the United States was ready to vote for the Declaration on the Granting of Independence for Colonial Countries and Peoples when a phone call from British Prime Minister Macmillan to President Eisenhower resulted in a last-minute switch to abstention.[17]

To implement the declaration the General Assembly established a Special Committee, which came to be known as the Special Committee of Twenty-four. Although the end of colonialism for a billion people was brought about largely through nonviolent means and, in most cases, with the acquiescence—ready or reluctant—of the administering powers, and although more than 90 percent of these people achieved self-determination *before* the establishment of the committee, in general, the attitude taken toward Western members in the committee has been one of antagonism and suspicion.

Resolutions have normally been worked out by a group of communist members and anti-Western African and Arab states. The latter, being militant and persistent, dominate the twelve-member Afro-Asian caucus of the committee. With the twelve Afro-Asian and four communist members committed, there is little disposition to compromise or negotiate within the committee. "Decisions" are presented on a take-it-or-leave-it basis to the three Latin American members and to the "other" (Western) members. (When the Special Committee of Twenty-four was at full strength there were five "others.") The Latin American members, in conceptual support of "decolonization," generally chose to back the decisions of the Afro-Asian-communist majority even when their explanations of vote would be more consistent with a negative than an affirmative vote. Sometimes, on flagrantly obnoxious proposals, they abstained. This had led to the lopsided votes and the lack of serious consultation or negotiation that characterizes the passage of most of the committee's resolutions.

Recommendations of the Special Committee of Twenty-four have usually gone on to become resolutions of the Fourth (Trusteeship and Non-Self-Governing Territories) Committee and the General Assembly. If such resolutions are changed from one year to the next, the change has usually been in the form of adding or inflating adjectives or inserting still more unattainable provisions.

For these reasons the United States concluded as early as January 1968 that it would be advisable to leave the Special Committee of Twenty-four. However, after informal consultation with the members it decided to remain on the committee, at least for a time, but to frankly express its views as to the committee's shortcomings and its earnest hope that there might be some improvement. The clear implication was that otherwise the United States would find little reason to justify continued participation in the committee's work. Accordingly, in February 1968 as the U.S. representative I outlined its misgivings about the Special Committee of Twenty-four. Specifically, I pointed out that solutions to the problems of dependent territories could be found only on the condition that the decision-making process be approached with no *a priori* assumptions about its outcome, that factual information be required, and that generalizations be avoided.[18] None of these conditions existed in the committee at that time.

Unfortunately, three more years then went by without any notable improvement. Praiseworthy efforts were made by two successive committee chairmen, Mahmoud Mestiri of Tunisia and Davidson Nicol of Sierra Leone, but the extremist coalition in the committee maintained its uncompromising domination.

The final straw for the United States was the failure of its efforts in 1970 to achieve meaningful consultation and negotiation on the program of action to be worked out by the committee in connection with the tenth anniversary of the Declaration of the Granting of Independence to Colonial Countries and Peoples.[19] The program was to set the guidelines for the committee's future work.

There was no real negotiation or consultation with either the United Kingdom or the United States. Instead, the program of action was drawn up in a working group whose proceedings were dominated by the representatives of the United Republic of Tanzania and the People's Republic of Bulgaria. Not only did this program carry forward all of the unworkable recommendations of previous sessions, but it added an endorsement of armed struggle and declared that "Member States shall render all necessary moral and material assistance to the peoples of colonial Territories in their struggle to attain freedom and independence."[20]

It was not the U.S. view that peoples should be denied the right to resort to any means at their disposal, including violence, if armed suppression by a colonial power required it. Indeed, the United States itself was obliged to resort to violence in order to gain independence. The difficulty lay in giving a general endorsement by the United Nations—an organization dedicated to peace—to such violence and in employing language that suggests that member states have an obligation to provide material assistance to violent action against other member states. Such action could hardly be reconciled with the requirements of the Charter of the United Nations.[21]

As the representative of the United States, I tried, first—and in vain—by attempting to encourage meaningful consultation and then by putting forward seventeen amendments, to achieve a text that would be practical, consistent with the Charter, and hopefully effective. Although these amendments were explained in the most conciliatory terms, all seventeen were summarily rejected. As a result, when put to the vote in the General Assembly the program of action was supported by only 86 members—about two-thirds of the membership but still an unusually low number for a resolution on colonial matters. Even such staunch anticolonialists as the Scandinavian countries and Austria were unable to vote in favor of this program of action, which thus lost much of its meaning.

This intransigent position appears even more ill advised in the light of the constructive program of action the Western members of the committee—Italy, Norway, the United Kingdom, and the United States—were prepared to support. Such a program would have emerged through acceptance either of the U.S. amendments or of the text presented by Italy to the committee[22] just before the program of action was rammed through by the majority on October 2, 1970.

The Italian proposal would have taken the Western countries much further than they had ever gone before in condemning the suppression of the legitimate aspirations of the colonial peoples and in setting forth a program of action designed to further the exercise of their right to self-determination, freedom, and independence. Although the proposal was presented by Italy in its own name, it had in fact been worked out by an informal caucus of representatives from Western countries, including Australia, France, New Zealand, Norway, the United Kingdom, and the United States. Had such a program been adopted, it could have served as a basis for genuine cooperation. Its rejection meant that the future activities of the committee would be in the same fruitless rut as in the past. It was therefore hard to escape the conclusion that the committee could not reform itself or be reformed. In these circumstances and after many years of effort the United States believed that it had no alternative but to withdraw, as it did on January 11, 1971.

In some ways extremist positions on anticolonial issues make life easier for the U.S. delegation. Not serving on the Special Committee of Twenty-four saves vast amounts of time and frustration. In the Fourth Committee of the General Assembly extremist resolutions pose no problem for the delegation; it can either abstain or vote against the resolution with a brief explanation, since positions on the perennial issues are well known. If, on the other hand, reasonable proposals are advanced, the delegation has to ask new instructions, and this often means a battle with certain entrenched positions in the State Department. But, comfortable or not, it is precisely in this difficult process of negotiating changes in policy and position that the best hope lies of achieving nonviolent solutions.

The African countries were aware of this fact and, as a consequence, increasingly brought the remaining problems in Africa, Zimbabwe (Rhodesia), Namibia (South-West Africa), and apartheid in South Africa before the Security Council where the major Western powers cannot escape their responsibility. Since the fifteen-member Security Council includes five Western members, three of which have the veto, and nine votes are required for a majority, there is more real negotiation in the Council. Britain, France, or the United States can veto any decision of the Council; however, if this veto is used with insensitivity and without any real effort to deal with the problem, one should not be surprised to see the African states press extremist language in the General Assembly and encourage wars of national liberation.

By the fall of 1970 Yost had decided that he would retire again the following spring. Realizing that he had little influence on major policy issues, Yost was not happy about his relationship with Nixon and Kissinger. Also, he enjoyed research and writing, which he had done for two years before Nixon appointed him, and wanted to return to it. Nevertheless, he was surprised and embarrassed when the news media revealed in November 1970 that the White House had sounded out Daniel Patrick Moynihan on taking over from Yost. Moynihan's patronizing statement that he did not want to be a party to humiliating Charles Yost did not help much. The problem was solved in November 1970 indirectly, when Lloyd Bentsen defeated Congressman George Bush for a Texas seat in the U.S. Senate, thus making Bush available to succeed Yost as permanent representative.

The cruel and clumsy leak about Moynihan did get Yost more media attention than he had before. As I told him, only half facetiously, it made him "box office." It probably improved the market for a syndicated column he undertook in early 1971. At the time of the leak, however, his private comment was that it convinced him he had been right in supporting the Democratic ticket.

NOTES

1. Richard Nixon, *RN: The Memoirs of Richard Nixon* (New York: Grosset & Dunlap, 1978), p. 338.
2. See, for example, Henry A. Kissinger, *American Foreign Policy* (New York: Norton, 1974), esp. pp. 51–98. See also John G. Stoessinger, *Henry Kissinger: The Anguish of Power* (New York: Norton, 1976).
3. Conversation with Samuel de Palma, March 8, 1978.
4. Charles W. Yost, *The Insecurity of Nations* (New York: Praeger, 1968), pp. 217–20.
5. Ibid., p. 77.

6. Ibid., p. 254.
7. Ibid., pp. 256–58.
8. Conversation with de Palma, March 8, 1978.
9. Conversation with Charles Yost, February 21, 1978, in Washington, D.C.
10. Conversation with de Palma, March 8, 1978.
11. Richard Nixon, *U.S. Foreign Policy for the 1970's*, a report to the U.S. Congress, February 25, 1971, pp. 123–32.
12. See S. M. Finger, "Breaking the Deadlock on U.N. Peacekeeping," *Orbis* (Summer 1973), pp. 385–98, for an account of the background and negotiations.
13. Nixon, *RN*, p. 201.
14. UN Security Council, Report of the Secretary-General on the Implementation of Security Council Resolution 340 (S/11052/Rev.1), October 27, 1973.
15. For a fuller discussion see S. M. Finger, "U.N. Peacekeeping and the U.S. National Interest" in S. M. Finger and J. R. Harbert, eds., *U.S. Policy in International Institutions* (Boulder, Colo.: Westview, 1978), pp. 71–77.
16. G. A. Res. 2676 (XXV), December 9, 1970.
17. Conversation with de Palma, March 8, 1978.
18. UN Doc. A/AC.109/SR. 574, pp. 5–7.
19. G. A. Res. 1514 (XV), December 14, 1960.
20. G. A. Res. 2621 (XXV), October 12, 1970, paragraph 3(2).
21. Charter considerations with respect to such actions are thoughtfully analyzed by Rupert Emerson in his article, "Self-Determination," *American Journal of International Law* 65, 3 (July 1971): 459–75.
22. UN Doc. A/8066, Annex 1.

CHAPTER XI

George Bush—A Future President at the UN

George H.W. Bush, who succeeded Yost in March 1971, was certainly one of the best-liked U.S. permanent representatives to serve at the UN. This was attributed to his engaging personality and assiduous cultivation of personal relationships, since the Nixon administration continued to show little real interest in the UN and, on African issues, moved away from the majority view.

Son of the late Prescott Bush, former U.S. senator from Connecticut, George Bush grew up in affluent surroundings, served as a hero Navy pilot in World War II, and went to Yale, where he was Phi Beta Kappa. He then moved to Texas, went into the business of oil exploration, and became independently wealthy. In 1968 he won a seat in the U.S. Congress, as a Republican. Two years later he was defeated in a race for the Senate and thus became available for the UN post.

Bush knew little about the UN when he arrived but was eager to learn and he worked hard at it. Although highly intelligent, he was not an intellectual in the sense that Yost was. Bush, like many politicians, preferred to get information and ideas through personal contacts rather than through extensive reading. This was sometimes a handicap when it came to understanding deep and complex problems but not in representing the United States on policies decided in Washington—as the pattern was during his tenure.

In personality and physical attributes, Bush reminded one of Lodge. He was tall, lean, handsome, and youthful-looking. He genuinely liked mixing with people and had a great knack for befriending them, as well as an apparently instinctive ability to avoid giving offense. He could argue persuasively and yet be a good listener. He made it a point not to act like a "big shot" (his words); he called on the ambassadors of smaller nations rather than make them come to him. He was, of course, equally courteous with the larger missions. He was punctilious about attending the many receptions and dinners hosted by other ambassadors, even though this involved a backbreaking social schedule. Both as host and as guest, he had great charm. He used the family farm in Connecticut as well as the official Waldorf Tower apartment to entertain widely and well. He was also very effective in giving public speeches around the country on behalf of the UN.

Bush, at my suggestion, initiated another informal way of entertaining foreign diplomats. I knew that his uncle, Herbert Walker, owned a major share of the New York Mets baseball team (Bush's full name is George Herbert Walker Bush). The Economic and Social Council was meeting in New York and I represented the United States there. I suggested that, instead of the usual formal cocktail party, we invite the Council members to an evening baseball game at Shea Stadium. Bush made the arrangements and we had a wonderful evening. Some of the diplomats brought their children, who received miniature baseball bats. It was most successful.

Bush relied heavily on career officers at both USUN and the State Department and worked very well with them. He did not replace any of the experienced officers at USUN with his people. Instead, when vacancies occurred he appointed, as his deputy, W. Tapley Bennett, Jr., a career foreign service officer who had been ambassador to the Dominican Republic and, as representative to the Economic and Social Council, Bernard Zagorin, a veteran Treasury Department official. Both had been recommended to Bush by the State Department. Bush did bring in Thomas Lias, his former congressional aide, to help him. Lias was not a barrier between the staff and Bush; rather, he helped Bush to organize his own paperwork and was a trusted adviser. (My personal relations with Bush were excellent, but, as I told him when he took over, I had already decided to leave in September 1971 to teach at the City University of New York.)

For all these qualities, Bush had little influence on American policy in the UN, which was generally defensive rather than innovative or supportive during his term. He was a very effective instrument of policy rather than an architect or influential partner in its formulation. His position was a result of the overall Nixon-Kissinger emphasis on great-power politics rather than the UN, the weak standing of Secretary Rogers, and the increasing tendency among the Third World majority to take positions that put the United States in an uncomfortable minority.

As for his relations with Nixon, Bush had this to say: "The appearance of closeness to the President, to the Secretary in those days, to the head of the NSC [Kissinger] was important in my ability to get things done. Frankly, there was more appearance than reality as far as the President went, although I did know him well and did have access to him when required." There is no evidence that Bush was able to initiate or change any significant policy by intervention with the President, but, for that matter, neither was Yost, Scali, or Moynihan.

In a note written in January 1978, Bush indicated that during his term, most policies and speeches were initiated in the State Department; this was in contrast with the practice under Lodge and Goldberg but tended to be the norm in cases where the permanent representative did not have considerable influence with the President. Bush was able to make some changes in the speeches, after clearing with State, but evidently none of substance. It is amazing that he was personally so popular among other delegates at a time when U.S. policy was so defensive and generally unsupportive; this is a tribute to his personal amiability and hard work in cultivating good relations. Given the Nixon-Kissinger mind-set, it was probably the best that could be done.

Bush was also a loyal team player. He believed the permanent representative should not appear to be another secretary of state and that the policymaking machinery in Washington must not be bypassed. In January 1978 he wrote me:

The UN represents but a part of our overall foreign policy initiatives and there only a small part of our foreign policy goals are enacted. Thus the Ambassador, even though in a very visible post, must coordinate with the Secretary of State and with IO and not try to run a separate ship. He has many contacts with Ambassadors and thus gets many insights into foreign policy; they should be cranked into the machinery. It confuses the hell out of our allies to have statements coming out of the UN or some other Embassy which may not agree with something the Secretary of State has said. The Ambassador should believe in the UN, want to strengthen it where possible. He owes the President, through the Secretary of State, his advice, his criticism, his best judgment; but when the decision is made he owes the President his support. No UN Ambassador can appear to run a foreign policy organization separate and apart from the State Department, certainly separate and apart from the policies determined by the President.

Seen in that light, he did his job very well indeed.

It is also worthy of note that, as President, Bush appointed a superb career diplomat, Thomas Pickering, as Permanent Representative. Pickering performed exceedingly well, particularly during the Persian Gulf crises, where Bush was outstandingly successful in using the UN to achieve American objectives. Getting a UN Security Council resolution authorizing the use of "all necessary means" to bring about the withdrawal of Iraqi forces from Kuwait (Resolution 678 of 28 November 1990) served Bush's purposes in three important ways: (1) it helped him to get authorization from the U.S. Senate; (2) it brought in eighteen allies in the military operation against Saddam Hussein, including ten Arab states; and (3) the United

States received $54 billion from other countries grateful for an operation that prevented Saddam from getting a choke hold on vital oil supplies from the Persian Gulf. Although Saddam has frustrated the Security Council in its efforts to verify destruction of his weapons of mass destruction, the situation would be much worse if Bush had not used the UN successfully in pushing his forces out of Kuwait.

CHINESE REPRESENTATION

Bush showed his loyalty very clearly at the twenty-sixth session of the General Assembly, his first as permanent representative. It had become increasingly clear that the People's Republic of China could not be kept out of the UN much longer. The Lodge Commission, in its report of April 26, 1971, had recommended a two-China policy. It stated that "all firmly established governments should be included in the UN system" but that the United States should "under no circumstances agree to the expulsion from the UN of the Republic of China on Taiwan"—in effect, a two-China policy.

Support for China-Taiwan had been eroding in the General Assembly. In 1970 a resolution to replace it with the People's Republic of China had majority support, 59 to 49, for the first time. It was not adopted because of a prior Assembly decision that such a move was an "important question" requiring a two-thirds majority, but even the number of countries supporting the "important question" resolution was declining. It was obvious in January 1971 that some changes in policy and tactics would be required to prevent China-Taiwan's expulsion. Also, the decision on change should have been made early so that friendly countries could be consulted, determine their own positions, perhaps make suggestions for change, and coordinate tactics for the General Assembly. Yet it was August before Washington gave the instructions to pursue a two-China policy at the forthcoming Assembly. The precious months lost would prove to be a serious handicap.

In fairness to Washington, there were serious problems in moving to a new policy. Both Peking and Taiwan rejected a two-China approach; each claimed to be the government of all of China. Chiang Kai-shek was adamant and he had some influential American supporters, mainly right-wing Republicans whom Nixon did not like to antagonize. It was probably for that reason that Nixon did not want to move before publication of the Lodge Commission Report, which recommended a two-China approach, in April 1971. The commission comprised people from a wide political spectrum, including stalwart, conservative Republicans, thus giving a degree of protective cover.

The commission, probably deliberately, left unanswered the question of representation on the Security Council. It was obviously unrealistic to expect Peking, which was in effective control of an area where 98 percent of China's people lived, to accept a situation where Taiwan continued to occupy China's seat on the Security Council, including veto privileges. Yet Washington was reluctant to bite the bullet.

Nixon had long since determined to improve communications and relations with the People's Republic of China. His historic visit to Peking a few months later (February 1972) had been preceded by three years of meticulous preparation beginning in his first few weeks of taking office. From mid-1969 onward the United States took steps to relax trade and travel restrictions, as a signal. Then, in official speeches and statements, such as Nixon's annual foreign policy reports, he signaled to the Chinese with increasing clarity the U.S. desire to reestablish and multiply contact and communication with Peking. In the spring of 1971 Peking began to show greater responsiveness; its invitation to an American table tennis team to visit China in April was one among many public signals. Then, on July 9, Kissinger secretly left Pakistan for a three-day visit to Peking, during which agreement was reached for the Nixon visit in order "to seek the normalization of relations between the two countries and to exchange views on questions of concern to the two sides."[1]

Finally, in August, the U.S. government came to an official decision that it would accept the seating of Peking in the Security Council as part of a two-China package. With the General Assembly opening only a few weeks later, there was little time to build support for the American position. Even NATO allies like Canada, Denmark, Iceland, Norway, and the United Kingdom, which recognized Peking but had supported the U.S. position on the "important question" resolution in earlier years, voted against the motion this time, while Belgium, Italy, and the Netherlands switched to abstentions. As a result, on October 25 the "important question" resolution was rejected for the first time; the vote was 55 to 59, with 15 abstentions.[2] The change in voting occurred despite the fact that this time the resolution reflected the new U.S. position. Instead of referring to any effort to change the representation of China as an "important question," the draft resolution would have required a two-thirds majority to expel a present member. Secretary Rogers, on October 4, and Ambassador Bush, on October 18, had noted that the Republic of China governs a population on Taiwan larger than the population of two thirds of the UN member states and argued that it would be just as unrealistic to deny them representation as to deny the People's Republic, "which exercises control over the largest number of people of all the world's governments," a seat on the Security Council. The Assembly went on to adopt the "Albanian" resolution recognizing the People's Republic as the sole representative of China, 76 to 35, with 17 abstentions. Its adoption touched off an enthusiastic and noisy demonstration, including dancing in the aisles by longtime, staunch supporters of Peking; this, in turn, led to bitter comments in Washington, strongly anti-UN majority in tone.

Was Nixon's anger about this result genuine and deep? It is hard to tell. In one way it was perfect for his domestic political position as well as his foreign policy aims. He had determined to improve relations with Peking, and his efforts were certainly helped by the fact that it was now in the United Nations. Peking's position on Taiwan made it doubtful that it would have accepted a two-China solution. Certainly Nixon's scheduled visit the following February would have met with a less cordial reception if the American position at the UN had prevailed. At the same time, by waging a losing battle against the expulsion of China-Taiwan and castigating the behavior of those who joyfully and publicly celebrated the event at the UN, Nixon deflected American right-wing denunciation from himself to them. His position was also helped in the United States by the Lodge Commission recommendation of April 1971.

Yet U.S. tactics had contributed substantially to the result. At USUN we felt in January 1971, as friendly countries pressed us, that an early U.S. decision on tactics at the Assembly was essential for building support. But the decision came in August. Kissinger's visit to Peking in July was a brilliant diplomatic stroke, but it did not help the U.S. position at the UN, especially at a time when Washington had made no decision yet on what to do at the General Assembly. Then Kissinger's visit to Peking in October, a week before the vote, while fully justified in terms of needed preparations for Nixon's historic trip, was bound to hurt U.S. chances of winning a majority for the "important question" resolution. At the time I suspected that a clever, devious Nixon had deliberately given priority to relations with Peking and, while ostensibly fighting to prevent Taiwan's expulsion, had actually contributed to that result. But in checking with Samuel de Palma, who was then assistant secretary of state for international organization affairs, I was informed that during the final days before the vote Nixon did authorize messages to heads of state and government urging support for the U.S. position. These were not first-person notes, the strongest kind, but they did swing at least one vote.[3]

With better tactics and more timely decisions it is probable that the United States could have kept China-Taiwan in the UN at the 1971 Assembly, considering the small margin on the "important question" resolution. Even so, the erosion would have continued, and in all likelihood the seating of Peking and ouster of Taiwan would have occurred soon thereafter, perhaps in 1972. In retrospect, it was probably better for the United States to lose. It is too bad, however, that President Nixon chose to make a scapegoat of the UN majority, thus fueling anti-UN sentiments in the Congress and among the American people.

Bush carried on with complete loyalty, dedication, and skill, doing his best to win in a hopeless situation. He made no public complaint about the delayed decisions or the timing of the Kissinger visits to Peking, either before or after the U.S. defeat. Even more remarkably, he cultivated relations with Peking's representatives at the UN with great success, so much so that he was later sent to Peking as chief of the U.S. liaison office there—the equivalent of ambassador, had relations been fully normalized.

NOTES

1. Nixon, *RN: The Memoirs of Richard Nixon* (New York: Grosset & Dunlap, 1978), pp. 17–18.

2. This paragraph is based on information in *U.S. Participation in the UN* (1970), The President's Report to Congress pp. 54–56.

3. Conversations with de Palma.

CHAPTER XII

Life after the Foreign Service

In the spring of 1971, I embarked on a new career. My wife Helen had been unhappy with the long hours I worked at the Mission, to which were added two hours daily commuting back and forth. I had tried to get a job with various investment banking firms, without success. Meanwhile, the Personnel Office in the State Department was putting pressure on me to take an overseas assignment after almost fifteen years in New York. If I got an overseas assignment, it was likely to be ambassador to some place like Ouagadougou in Africa, not a thrilling prospect. Then I saw an advertisement in the *New York Times* indicating that a branch of the City University of New York was hiring additional professors. I wrote a letter of application for a post as Professor of Political Science. The college turned out to be the Staten Island Community College. I was called for an interview with a departmental committee of five professors, who recommended my appointment.

I was very happy with the appointment. I taught four courses, each of which met three hours per week—a total of twelve hours. Of course, I spent more than 30 additional hours per week seeing students, preparing classes, devising and grading examinations, and research and writing, but the bulk of that time I could work at home, which made Helen happy. Moreover, since my teenage years at Ohio University, I had dreamed of being a professor. Now, almost 40 years later, my dream was being realized. And I really enjoyed teaching!

It was also a good time for me to retire from the Foreign Service. I had served 26 years and, combined with my Army service of 3 years and 15 months of accumulated sick leave, I was eligible for a 30-year service pension. At age 56, I was still young enough to embark on a new career.

George Bush, our Permanent Representative at the time, and later President Bush, was reluctant to see me go. I liked and respected him, but Helen's strong needs, and my own readiness to take up a new career prevailed. At one point he suggested that I wait until January, when the job market would be better. I pointed out that, in the academic world, hiring took place in the spring and the job began in September. We remained on very friendly terms and, two years later, when I established the Ralph Bunche Institute on the United Nations, he agreed to serve on the Board.

In due course the Staten Island Community College merged with Richmond College to become a four-year institution, the College of Staten Island. I enjoyed teaching there and had a good rapport with the students and my faculty colleagues.

Then came a step that brought me part-time to the Graduate School of the City University of New York on 42nd Street. While I was still at the Mission, my friend, Richard Gardner, then professor of law at Columbia University, asked whether I would be willing to direct an institute on the UN at Columbia. I said I would, but then came the problem of raising money to fund the institute. We had pledges for about half the sum required but no more was forthcoming. Accordingly, the idea was dropped, but it stayed in my head. Why not, I reasoned, establish such an institute at the CUNY Graduate School, which was a ten-minute walk from the UN?

I went to sell the idea to Dr. Harold Proshansky, then President of the Graduate School. I was lucky in that he invited the Dean of Special Programs, Dr. Benjamin Rivlin, to join us. Rivlin was a strong supporter of the UN who had worked with Ralph Bunche, a former undersecretary general at the UN. He helped greatly to gain Proshansky's support, and the institute was established.

It was Ben's idea to name the institute after the late Ralph Bunche, the most distinguished American official to serve at the UN. We went to see his widow, Ruth, who approved, and the Ralph Bunche Institute on the UN was launched. As Director, I had to spend part of my time at the Graduate School. I also taught classes there. As a result, I became an "island hopper," driving from Long to Staten to Manhattan and back to Long. I also had the motivation and opportunity to write two books, edit and write introductions to five, and contribute more than 80 articles to professional journals.

DIPLOMATIC INVOLVEMENT

My shift to academia did not end my involvement with international politics. As Director of the Ralph Bunche Institute on the United Nations and as teacher of courses on the UN, I kept up my involvement with issues and people there. I also organized seminars involving UN personnel with students, faculty, and businesspeople, as well as UN internships for students.

In addition, I continued to concern myself with the plight of the 2,200 Jews remaining in Iraq. While still at the Mission, I was approached by former Iraqi Jews, now settled in the United States, who had relatives endangered in Iraq. Saddam Hussein had just hanged eleven Jews in Baghdad and no one knew where it would stop. One of them came to see me on the day Bill Jorgensen was to run the story on TV Channel 5. I immediately called Ralph Bunche to suggest that he watch, and he and Secretary General U Thant both did. They were deeply concerned and Thant called in the French ambassador to suggest that his government intervene in Baghdad, which they did. There is no evidence that the intervention had any impact.

My next effort was more promising. I learned that Sadruddin Aga Khan, the UN High Commissioner for Refugees, was in Washington and I called him there. He turned out to be both interested and sympathetic. Moreover, he had a special entrée to Baghdad. His family headed the Ismaeli sect of Islam, which had many adherents in Iraq; consequently, he went there periodically to maintain contacts with the Ismaelis. While he was there, Saddam used him as an intermediary to propose a deal with the Shah of Iran. (Sadruddin carried an Iranian passport.) There was a dispute over the Shatt-al-Arab, an inlet of the Persian Gulf with Iraq claiming the entire inlet and Iran claiming half of it. Saddam would agree to the Iranian position if the Shah would stop helping the Kurds in northern Iraq, who were fighting for independence. Sadruddin conveyed the message and the deal was made. He then used the dialogue to bring up the plight of the Iraqi Jews, urging Saddam to let them go. In due time, in fact, all who wanted to leave were able to do so, escaping through the Kurdish area of the north, usually with bribery. The escape came while I was a professor, but my wife, Helen, and I were involved the entire time, being available to the relatives of the endangered Jews at all hours of the day and night. Helen made a particular effort to get stories about their plight into American and Canadian newspapers. The successful exodus of 2,000 Jews from Iraq was the most gratifying event of my entire career.

In gratitude, the American Committee for the Rescue of Iraqi Jews offered to give a dinner in my honor at the Plaza Hotel. I told them I would accept only if they would honor Helen as well. They agreed and, in fact, we balstered the position of Iraqi Jewish womanhood in the process. On the night of the dinner, the platform held not only Helen and me, but the wives of all their officials alongside their husbands. It was a beautiful and elegant affair, with flattering tributes being made. Helen responded with a gracious statement lauding the courage and fortitude of the escapees and their families.

Another involvement followed on the adoption by the UN General Assembly of a resolution equating Zionism with racism, which shocked not only Israel, but Jews all around the world. I attended a meeting at the Synagogue Council of America, along with representatives of the major American Jewish organizations. One speaker after another vented rage against the UN and the ungrateful African countries, many of which had been aided by Israel. I shared the anger and outrage, but my background as a diplomat suggested an added dimension. Hence, when I got up to speak, I commented that getting these feelings out was good for psychic health, but did not constitute a policy. In the long run, Israel and the United States needed good relations with the African and Asian countries and our goal should be to develop those relationships.

Max Melamet, the representative of the World Jewish Congress (WJC), was impressed with my remarks, and suggested to Philip Klutznick, then President of the World Jewish Congress, that I be engaged as a consultant. (He did not know that Phil and I had worked closely together under Stevenson.) Phil endorsed the idea and I became a WJC consultant for a decade. I organized lunches with UN representatives, principally from Africa and Asia, where we could subtly get across the message that their support of resolutions unjustly equating Zionism with racism would make it difficult for the United States to support economic programs they wanted. I got a lucky break right at the beginning. Our first event included Cyrus Vance, who shortly thereafter was named Secretary of State. Delegates apparently concluded that I had a pipeline to God, or at least the President of the United States. The occasions multiplied, with alternate hosting by the delegates and the WJC, and I think we made an impact. In fact, some years later, the General Assembly rescinded the resolution equating Zionism with racism.

I continued as a consultant to the WJC after Edgar Bronfman succeeded Klutznick. I arranged lunches with the Soviet ambassador and the Secretary General. Now Bronfman and his two able deputies, Israel Singer and Elan Steinberg, have succeeded in having meaningful contacts with prime ministers, foreign ministers, and ambassadors from many countries and I have become an admiring onlooker.

Subsequently, I became involved in an intervention of a much more personal nature. My old friend, Bill Korey, a scholarly official with B'nai Brith, came to see me about the plight of Valery Panov, a Jewish dancer with the Leningrad Kirov ballet. For ethnic reasons Panov was excluded from dancing with the Kirov company and was apparently desperately unhappy with his enforced idleness. Korey appealed to me to try to get Panov out.

I called an old acquaintance, Evgeny Makeev, who was then Deputy Permanent Representative at the Soviet mission. When I made my pitch on Panov's behalf, Makeev with a note taker present, proceeded to upbraid me for intervening in internal Soviet affairs and said he would not have agreed to see me if he had known what I wanted. If nothing else, this covered his rear end in Moscow. I suspect he made sure that my message got through to Moscow, along with Makeev's bawling me out. Whether this was so or not, Panov did get out shortly thereafter.

At age 70 I was obliged to retire from CUNY because of legislation then prevailing. Ironically, Helen, who had been pleading with me to retire for many years, died suddenly at the time my retirement became effective. To fill the void, I continued working at the Ralph Bunche Institute. I went through the motions of living, but a part of me died with her. Going to the Ralph Bunche Institute helped to fill my days.

Then, three months after Helen's death, I received a call from New York University (NYU) asking whether I would like to teach a course on international terrorism. (A few years earlier I had written some articles on the subject and coedited a book on it.) At that point I had decided that there was little reason for me to live on Long Island when most of my interests, including the Council on Foreign Relations and the UN, were in Manhattan. I knew NYU owned many apartment buildings and thought I might get an apartment.

As an adjunct professor I did not get the apartment, but something infinitely more precious, Annette, who eventually became my wife. Annette was Director of Modern Language Education and International Studies at NYU. Coming from France to the United States as a refugee from the Nazis, she arrived in late August 1943 without a word of English and having been out of school for two and a half years. Not knowing anything better to do, the school put her in a class for retarded children. Three and a half years later she graduated as the high school valedictorian! She did brilliantly at Brooklyn College (Phi Beta Kappa) and eventually earned her Ph.D. with distinction at NYU. She became a professor first at Columbia and then NYU. She has an eloquence in English that far surpasses the language skills of 95 percent of people born here.

RETROSPECTIVE

I wonder what my life would have been like if my trainee had not made a chance remark that I should be in the diplomatic service. I probably would have had a successful business in Houston and made a lot of money. But I have no regrets about my choice of career.

Being a Foreign Service Officer was a constant education—learning about new countries, their people and their languages. The job at the United Nations involved very long hours, working much harder than in private business and earning much less. But it was such a great privilege to help design policies and programs that could contribute to the pursuit of world peace and well-being. It was, to use Arthur Goldberg's phrase, a struggle that had to be won "inch by agonizing inch." There is no quick, magic formula. It is a persistent struggle, with many defeats and setbacks.

But it is a struggle that must be waged, regardless of difficulties and frustrations.

Wars continue to break out, despite our best efforts. But working through the UN, we have managed to bring many of them to an end. Also, the spread of nuclear weapons has been limited. Massive poverty and disease continue to be widespread, but the UN system has made highly significant contributions to increasing food production, alleviating famine, helping children, combating disease, and fostering economic development. Much, much more remains to be done and the outlook is grim. Yet, in the absence of diplomacy and the UN, the situation would be much worse. This is not the time to give up. Rather, it is the time to rededicate ourselves to the struggle for peace and the well-being of humankind.

CHAPTER XIII

A Foreign Service for the 21st Century

As we look ahead to the new century, it is clear that new challenges will appear. The dominant issue of the cold war is now history, but we are faced with serious new challenges. The thrust of globalization is making the economic aspects of foreign policy ever more important. The increasing incidence of civil war, the egregious violation of human rights, and the proliferation of ethnic insurgencies are a serious challenge to the making of coherent policy. How can the U.S. Foreign Service prepare to meet these challenges?

First, I believe that the practices that have given us such a competent Foreign Service should be continued. In 26 years of service, I developed a great respect for my colleagues and felt proud to be part of such an elite service. I believe that appointments should continue to be made on the basis of the difficult, challenging examinations, both written and oral. Promotions should continue to be made on the basis of superiors' evaluations, supplemented by the observations of Foreign Service inspectors. Officers who do not merit promotion during a given period of years should continue to be eased out of the service, especially during their early years when they are still young enough to make a transition without undue hardship. Indeed, recent assessments by the Department of State, assisted by two major consulting firms, STG and McKinsey and Company, suggest that the Foreign Service should offer faster advancement to the best and move aside more of the weaker performers.

The State Department's report, based on these assessments, reached the following conclusions:

- there is an intense war for talent going on due to demographic factors in the job market and the increasing mobility of the workforce. (Corporations can offer much higher salaries to competent people who want to live abroad.);
- the Department continues to attract talented individuals because its work is seen as exciting and inspiring, and it is seen as having a talented workforce;
- but the Department lacks a talent mind-set: 70 percent of our senior managers did not rank talent management among their top five priorities. As a result, the rank and file view the Department as a poorly managed organization;
- the Department fails to differentiate people sufficiently based on performance. It does not offer fast enough advancement to the best and brightest, nor does it move aside enough of the weaker performers;
- although geographic mobility is a drawing card for talent, the Department does not do enough to meet the challenges faced by dual-career couples.[1]

The report also emphasizes the need for better management of talent. It points out that corporations constantly, conscientiously train their employees in management techniques and practices. Such training has not been emphasized sufficiently in the State Department and the Foreign Service. Now the Director General of the Foreign Service and the Foreign Service Institute have developed a leadership continuum for both the foreign and civil service.[2] The Director General, Ambassador Edward W. Gnehm, Jr. has proposed the development of a system of incentives so that foreign service officers will be motivated to take advantage of leadership and management training.

Gnehm further suggests the use of "headhunters" to assist spouses who want to pursue their professions overseas. In my own Foreign Service days, wives were generally unable to pursue careers, but they often did important volunteer work without pay. This practice has had to be abandoned as the two-career family has become the norm. Consequently, a stronger effort to assist professional spouses is urgently needed.

Another area where Gnehm has taken significant action is speeding up the appointment process. This has been applied particularly to qualified people in categories where the Foreign Service has its worst deficits—office management, information management, and information management technology. Given the competition for talent from corporations, prospective employees are no longer willing to wait for long periods before an appointment decision is made.[3]

Another area of progress has been the development of computer literacy among Foreign Service officers. I am informed that the Foreign Service Institute now provides computer training before an officer is sent abroad. This should not only make for better informed, more effective officers but also reduce the amount of secretarial assistance per officer, thus reducing payroll.

The State Department and the Foreign Service are also adapting well to the addition to the Department of the Arms Control and Disarmament Agency (ACDA) and the U.S. Information Agency (USIA). The new structure, mandated by Congress, should help in the integration of arms control and information policies into the overall development and execution of U.S. foreign policy.

In addition to the improvements now being introduced, there are two areas of major importance to the United States that I believe require new directions for the Foreign Service. The first is globalization, which has brought economic issues to the forefront of national concerns.[4] Consequently, I believe that Foreign Service officers should be given much more training and education in business and economics. In my own case, I found an academic year of studying graduate-level economics at Harvard to be enormously valuable in my subsequent service—but that training took place at my initiative, not the State Department's.

Another area that should get more attention is Chinese studies. The Foreign Service has done a superb job in preparing officers for service in Russia and work on Russian problems. A formidable number of officers have developed fluency in Russian and deep understanding of Russia—men like George Kennan, who was responsible for developing the policy of containment that was the cornerstone of American foreign policy for half a century. Now China has become an increasingly important player on the world scene, and it behooves us to develop officers with first-rate competence in Chinese language, history, and politics. We have serious differences with China over human rights violations, especially in Tibet, its economic policies that have led to a huge trade imbalance in China's favor, and its efforts to assert control over the South China Sea. There is also the overhanging threat to Taiwan. Dealing with these major problems will require a substantial number of additional officers who know the Chinese language and understand China.

There is one very important problem that cannot be solved by the State Department or its Foreign Service, i.e., the security of American personnel and buildings abroad. Our vulnerability was highlighted again in August 1998 by the terrorist bombings of our embassies in Dar es Salaam and Nairobi, with a tragic loss of numerous lives of American and local personnel. Serving abroad has long been dangerous and is getting more so. Much more could and should be done to bolster the security of our embassies and consulates abroad. Unfortunately, Congress has not appropriated enough money to do the job at many of our installations. This prolongs an unconscionable risk to our people serving abroad. The necessary funds should and must be appropriated.

Congress and the American people must realize that a first-class American diplomacy is as important as a first-class military. Our diplomacy has averted or stopped many wars and developed programs of great importance to American welfare and development. There are still enormous challenges ahead. Only the best will do, in both our military establishment and our diplomacy.

NOTES

1. *Department Notice*, August 18, 1999, p. 2.
2. Ibid, p. 3.
3. Remarks by the Director General of the Foreign Service on Foreign Service Day, May 7, 1999.
4. Thomas L. Friedman, *The Lexus and the Olive Tree* (New York: Farrar, Straus and Giroux, 1995).

Bibliography

Acheson, Dean. *Power and Diplomacy.* Cambridge, Mass: Harvard University Press, 1958.
Ball, George W. *Diplomacy for a Crowded World.* Boston: Atlantic–Little, Brown, 1976.
Bennett, A. Leroy. *International Organizations, Principles and Issues.* 5th ed. Englewood Cliffs, N.J.: Prentice-Hall, 1991.
Boudreau, Thomas E. *Sheathing the Sword: The UN Secretary General and the Prevention of International Conflict.* Westport, Conn.: Greenwood Press, 1991.
Boyd, James. *United Nations Peacekeeping Operations: A Military and Political Appraisal.* New York: Praeger, 1971.
Bull, Odd. *War and Peace in the Middle East: The Experience and Views of a UN Observer.* Boulder, Colo: Westview, 1973.
Bush, George, and Brent Sloweroft. *A World Transformed.* New York: Alfred A. Knopf, 1998.
Claude, Inis. *Swords into Plowshares.* 4th ed. New York: Random House, 1971.
Davis, Kenneth S. *The Politics of Honor. A Biography of Adlai E. Stevenson.* New York: Putnam, 1967.
Ducharek, Ivo. *Nations and Men.* 3rd ed., Hinsdale, Ill: Dryden, 1975.
Fabian, Larry. *Soldiers without Enemies: Preparing the UN for Peacekeeping.* Washington, D.C.: Brookings Institution, 1971.
Finger, S.M., ed. *The New World Balance and Peace in the Middle East.* New York: Associated Universities Press, 1975.
Finger, S.M., and J.R. Harbert. *U.S. Policy in International Institutions.* Boulder, Colo.: Westview, 1978.
Finger, S.M., and Arnold Saltzman. *Bending with the Wind; Kurt Waldheim and the United Nations.* New York: Praeger 1990.

Gati, Toby Trister. *The U.S., the U.N., and the Management of Global Change*. New York: New York University Press, 1983.
Goldberg, Dorothy K. *A Private View of a Public Life*. New York: Charterhouse, 1975.
Gordenker, Leon. *The UN Secretary General and the Maintenance of Peace*. New York: Columbia University Press, 1967.
Hadwen, John G., and Johan Kaufmann. *How United Nations Decisions Are Made*. Leyden: A. W. Sijthoff, 1960.
Henkin, Louis. *The Age of Rights*. New York: Columbia University Press, 1990.
Holbrooke, Richard. *To End a War*. New York: Random House, 1998.
Holsti, Ole R. *Public Opinion and American Foreign Policy*. Ann Arbor: University of Michigan Press, 1996.
Kapstein, Ethan, and Michael Mastanduno. *Unipolar Politics: Realism and State Strategies after the Cold War*. New York: Columbia University Press, 1990.
Kissinger, Henry A. *American Foreign Policy*. New York: W. W. Norton, 1974.
Kull, Steven, and J.M. Destler. *The Myth of a New Isolationism*. Washington, D.C.: Brookings Institution Press, 1999.
Lake, Anthony. *The "Tar Baby" Option*. New York: Columbia University Press, 1976.
Lall, Arthur S. *The United Nations and the Middle East Crisis*. New York: Columbia University Press, 1968.
LeFever, Ernest W. *Crisis in the Congo*. Washington, D.C.: Brookings Institution, 1965.
Lipset, Seymour Martin. *American Exceptionalism: A Double-Edged Sword*. New York: W. W. Norton, 1996.
Lodge, Henry Cabot. *As It Was: An Inside View of Politics in the 50's and 60's*. New York: W. W. Norton, 1976.
Luck, Edward C. *Mixed Messages: American Politics and International Organization, 1919–1999*. Washington, D.C.: Brookings Institution Press, 1999.
Martin, John B. *Adlai Stevenson of Illinois*. Garden City, N.Y.: Doubleday, 1976.
Nicholas, H. G. *The United Nations as a Political Institution*. London: Oxford University Press, 1971.
Nixon, Richard. *RN: The Memoirs of Richard Nixon*. New York: Grosset & Dunlap, 1978.
Nordlinger, Eric A. *Isolationism Reconfigured: American Foreign Policy for a New Century*. Princeton, N.J.: Princeton University Press, 1995.
O'Brien, Conor Cruise. *To Katanger and Back*. New York: Simon & Schuster, 1962.
Rivlin, Benjamin, ed. *Ralph Bunche: The Man and His Times*. New York: Holmes & Meier, 1990.
Rosenau, James. *Turbulence in World Politics*. Princeton, N.J.: Princeton University Press, 1990.
Russell, Ruth B. *The United Nations and United States Security Policy*. Washington, D.C.: Brookings Institution, 1968.
Schlesinger, Arthur M., Jr. *A Thousand Days: John F. Kennedy in the White House*. Boston: Houghton Mifflin, 1965.
Sorenson, Theodore. *Kennedy*. New York: Harper & Row, 1965.
Stoessinger, John G. *The United Nations and the Superpowers*. New York: Random House, 1965.

Touval, Saadia. *The Peace Brokers: Mediators in the Arab-Israeli Conflict*. Princeton, N.J.: Princeton University Press, 1982.
Urquhart, Brian. *Hammarskjold*. New York: Knopf, 1972.
Wicker, Tom. *JFK and LBJ: The Influence of Personality upon Politics*. New York: Morrow, 1968.
Yost, Charles W. *The Insecurity of Nations*. New York: Praeger, 1968.
Zakaria, Fareed. *From Wealth to Power: The Unusual Origins of America's World Role*. Princeton, N.J.: Princeton University Press, 1998.

Index

Acheson, Dean, 40, 107
Adoula, Cyrille, 55
Aga Khan, Sadruddin, 151
Agnelli, Gianni, 54
Alsop, Stewart, 61
American Photograph Corporation, 2
American Joint Distribution Committee, 5
Anderson, Eugenie, 101
Aqaba, 109–110
Arab-Israeli dispute, 38–40
Arbenz, Jacob, 43
Arkadiev, Georgi, 37
Article 19, 69–75, 76–79, 102–104
Atherton, Roy, 7
Azores, 52

Bailey, Pearl, 33
Baker, John C., 29
Balaguer, Joaquin, 68
Balazs, Bill, 15
Ball, George, 53, 121–123
Barco, James, 29
Baroody, Jamil, 123
Barromi, Joel, 111
Bartlett, Charles, 61

Battle of the Bulge, 3
Bay of Pigs, 57–58
Beichman, Arnold, 44n.17
Bender, Albert, 51, 69
Benton, William, 50
Berman, Harold, 18
Berman, Jacob, 13
Bernardo, Hector, 82
Bingham, Jonathan, 51
Black, Eugene, 70
Blancke, Wendell, 22
Bloch, Henry, 35
Bong (Souvannivong), 22
Boyd, James, 100
Brezhnev doctrine, 67, 123
Bronfman, Edgar, 152
Bruce, David, 10
Budo, Halim, 77
Buffum, William, 101
Bunche, Ralph, 29, 56, 75–76, 151
Bundy, McGeorge, 53, 85
Bush, George H.W., 141–146
Bush, Prescott, 141

Caradon, Lord, 115
Carter, Rudolph, 100

Casson, Peter, 84
Castro, Fidel, 57–62
Chinese representation, 144–147
Church, Frank, 33
CIA, 15
City University of New York, 149
Cleveland, Harlan, 79, 82
Cochran, Bert, 61
COCOM, 19
Commission on Human Rights, 51
Committee of Twenty Four, 135–138
Congo, 54–57
Cordier, Andrew, 96
Cuba, 58–62
Czechoslovakia, 121–123

d'Arboussier, Gabriel, 84
Davies, John, 34
de Palma, Samuel, 130–131, 147
Dick, Jane, 51
Dirksen, Everett, 25
Dobrynin, Anatoly, 114–116
Dominican crisis, 67–69
Dulles, John Foster, 21, 38, 39, 40
Dunne, Irene, 33

ECOSOC (Economic and Social Council), 42
Egypt, 38–40, 110–116
Eighteen Nation Disarmament Committee, 118–119
Eisenhower, Dwight, 28, 38, 40
EPTA (Expanded Program of Technical Assistance), 31
EURATOM (European Atomic Energy Community), 118–119

FAO (Food and Agriculture Organization), 37
Fedorenko, Nikolai, 111–114, 116, 122
First Amendment, 116–117
Flood, Curt, 120
Ford, Henry II, 33
Ford Foundation, 84
Fortas, Abe, 92
Foster, William H., 118–119
Fourth Committee, Decolonization, 135–138

Fredericks, Wayne, 106
Freeman, Orville, 37
Fritchey, Clayton, 51, 52

Galbraith, Kenneth, 17
Gardner, Richard, 18, 79, 83, 150
Gnehm, Edward W. Jr., 156
Goldberg, Arthur J., 91–116, 117–120
Goldberg, Dorothy, 102
Goldschmidt, Arthur, 101

Haberler, Gottfried, 18
Hammarskjöld, Dag, 42, 43
Hanes, John, 32
Hansen, Alvin, 17
Harriman, Averell, 118
Hayek, Jiri, 122
Hebrew Immigrant Aid Society (HIAS), 5
Heuss, Theodor, 7
Hoffman, Paul G., 30
Holmes, John, 84
Humphrey, George, 30
Humphrey, Hubert, 96–97

International Development Association (IDA), 34
International Atomic Energy Agency, (IAEA), 118
International Court of Justice (ICJ), 71, 103
Iraq, 151
Israel, 38–40, 110–116, 152

Javits, Jacob, 134
Jebb, Gladwyn, 45n.18
Johnson, Lyndon, 66–67, 113
Judd, Walter, 31, 32

Kasavubu, Joseph, 55
Kennedy, Jacqueline, 4, 8
Kennedy, John F., 47, 48, 49
Kennedy, Robert, 54
Kissinger, Henry, 130–131
Klutznick, Philip M., 50, 51, 69, 70, 152
Korey, Bill, 152

Index

Khrushchev, Nikita, 41
Kuwait, 143–144
Kuznetsov, Vasily, 119

Laos, 21–25
Lavrichenko, Soviet representative, 82
Lias, Thomas, 142
Lloyd Rupert, 9, 10
Lodge, Henry Cabot, 27, 30, 40, 41
Lumumba, Patrice, 54–55

Makeev, Evgeny, 152–153
Malaysia, 35, 36
Malik, Jacob, 132
Mansfield, Mike, 25
Marof, Achkar, 54
Martin, John B., 48–49, 53–54
Mayo, Walter, 33
Mayobre, Antonio, 68
McCain, Admiral John S., 99–100
McCloy, John, 59
McNamara, Robert, 53
Meany, George, 33, 36
Meier, Reinhold, 7
Melamet, Max, 152
Mendelevich, Lev, 132
Mestiri, Mahmoud, 136
Mobutu, Sese Seko, 54
Moore, Alex, 24

Nabrit, James M., 98
Narasimhan, C. V., 84
Nasser, Gamel, 109
National Security Agency, 95
Nhouy (Abhay), 22
Nicholas, H. G., 78
Nicol, Davidson, 136
Nixon, Richard, 36, 41, 42
Noyes, Charles, 51
NPT (Nuclear Non-proliferation Treaty), 118–120

O'Sheel, Pat, 15
OAS (Organization of American States), 67–69
ONUC (UN Operation in the Congo), 54–57, 69–72
Organization of African Unity, 67

Panov, Valery, 152–153
Pauker, Ana, 13
Pearson, Lester, 39–40
Pedersen, Richard, 73, 99
Pelcovits, Nathan, 131
Phoui (Sananikone), 22
Plimpton, Francis T. P., 50, 98
Proshansky, Harold, 150

Quaison-Sackey, Alex, 75

Rabb, Maxwell, 27
Rakosi, Matyas, 13, 15
Ravndal, Christian, 15
Resolution 242, 114–116
Resolution 1219, 32–33
Rhodesia, 104–108
Rivlin, Benjamin, 76
Rockefeller, John D. III, 84
Rogers, William, 33, 116–117, 130
Roosevelt, James, 96
Roosevelt, Eleanor, 51
Rostow, Walt, 53, 68, 93
Rusk, Dean, 49
Russell, Ruth, 78

Sadat, Anwar, 7
Schlesinger, Arthur, 48
Sears, Mason, 29
Sebon, Blair, 64
Shriver, Sargent, 128
Singer, Israel, 152
Sisco, Joseph, 101, 106–107
Six-Day War, 108–116
Slansky, Rudolph, 13
Smith, Ian, 105
Solomon, Pat, 115
Sopiee, Mohammed, 35, 36
Sorenson, Theodore, 85n.2
Sosa Rodriguez, Carlos, 73
Souphannavong, 23
Souvanna Phouma, 23
Special Committee on Peacekeeping Operations, 103, 131–134
Special Fund, 31–35
Special Projects Fund, 31–32
Stalin, Joseph, 16
State Department, U.S., 6

Steinberg, Elan, 152
Stevenson, Adlai, 23, 47–69, 85
Suez Canal, 38, 39, 40
SUNFED (Special UN Fund for Economic Development), 30–33
Sweden (Conference on Environment), 123

Tabor, Hans, 112
Temple, Shirley, 33
Thant, U, 55–56, 64–65
Tree, Marietta, 51
Truman, Harry, 5
Tshombe, Moise, 54–57

UN Capital Development Fund (UNCDF), 33, 34
UN Development Decade, 3, 79–82
UN Development Program, 33, 34, 35
UN Economic and Social Council, 42
UN Emergency Force in the Middle East, 39–40, 132
UN High Commissioner for Refugees, 151
UN Institute for Training and Research, 82–84
UNDOF, 134
UNEF, 39, 40, 108–109, 133
United Nations Development Decade, 79–82
Uniting for Peace resolution, 113
Universal Declaration of Human Rights, 51
UNTSO (UN Truce Supervision Organization), 108, 113
U.S. Foreign Service, 2–6, 155–158
U.S. Information Agency (USIA), 157
USS Pueblo, 117–118

Valenti, Jack, 91
Vance, Cyrus, 152
Vogeler, 13
Vreeland, Frederick, 100

Wadsworth, James J., 29
Wiggins, James Russell, 123
Wilken, David, 42
Williams, John, 17
Williams, Mennen, 55, 106
World Bank (International Bank for Reconstruction and Development), 34
World Food Program, 36, 37
World Jewish Congress, 152
Wright, Nonnie, 30, 34, 89

Yorty, Sam, 41
Yost, Charles, 22, 23, 50, 111, 127–134, 138

Zafrula Khan, Mohammed, 73

About the Author

SEYMOUR M. FINGER is Senior Fellow, Ralph Bunche Institute on the United Nations and President of the Institution on Mediterranean Affairs. He is Adjunct Professor of Political Science at the Graduate Center of the City University of New York and New York University, Visiting Professor at Georgetown University, and Professor Emeritus of Political Science at the College of Staten Island. He served for 26 years as a career diplomat in the U.S. Foreign Service, rising through the ranks to become an American Ambassador at the UN, where he had a major role in the establishment of the UN Development Program and the World Food Program. Ambassador Finger published seven earlier books, including *Bending with the Winds: Kurt Waldheim and the United Nations* (Praeger, 1990).